(3741)   £8.00

HAMPSHIRE PRIVIES

by

IAN FOX

C   SIDE BOOKS

NEWBURY · BERKSHIRE

First published 1997
© Ian Fox 1997

All rights reserved. No reproduction
permitted without the prior permission
of the publisher:

COUNTRYSIDE BOOKS
3 Catherine Road
Newbury, Berkshire

ISBN 1 85306 470 X

Produced through MRM Associates Ltd., Reading
Printed by Woolnough Bookbinding Ltd., Irthlingborough

CONTENTS

FOREWORD

Our house didn't have a privy. We did, however, have a WC outside the back door, next to the coal shed, with a high, cast-iron cistern and a paraffin stove to keep it from freezing-up in the winter.

This was probably the nearest thing to enjoying the pleasures of a privy without its disadvantages. It was a different world out there, a sanctuary for reading, thinking, or simply for solitude (there was another one indoors, so no-one was kept waiting). It also provided a great bolt-hole to avoid doing the washing-up.

I endured the rigours of the authentic British thunderbox only briefly, at army camps with the school cadet corps. One particularly traumatic moment came when, feeling unwell, hardly had I begun to perform before I heard voices outside, caught the suffocating stink of the honeycart, felt fresh air around my nether regions and realised the bucket had been whipped away. Those few moments of clenched-buttock sweating before it was replaced were some of the longest in my young life.

Thus I can claim at least some shared experience with the people whose memories feature in this book. It is intended as a tribute to them and to those little private places that featured so vitally in their lives.

I asked for their help and they responded magnificently. Their letters were a joy, and as I toured the county to flush out and photograph the few remaining privies, I encountered nothing but genuine interest and a sense of satisfaction that the story was being recorded for future generations.

There isn't the space to thank everyone by name but any list of favourites would have to include the gracious lady who unwittingly gave me one gloriously surreal moment.

Everything about her spoke of genteel upbringing. Her courtesy belonged to another age. Bees murmured in the summer

Is this Hampshire's oldest surviving privy? Built of cob and thatch, it stands beneath lime trees in the garden of a listed 16th-century farmhouse in Damerham. Its seat has long been destroyed.

flowers as we drank tea from thin china cups in the garden of her exquisitely English cottage. She told me in cultured tones of the 'night soil men' who emptied the buckets when she was young. Did her family, I ventured, give them a nickname? The lavender lorry, perhaps, or the bed of roses?

She frowned in fragrant concentration. Then, earnestly: 'Do you know, I cannot remember us calling it anything other than The Shit Cart.'

To her, to others who helped, to my wife for her patience, support and encouragement, and to everyone who ever perched in a privy, this book is dedicated. Should you be reading it in the smallest room, please do not tear out pages except in extreme emergency. You will probably find toilet paper is provided. Or newspaper squares.

IAN FOX

[1]

Privy Progress

Where to do it and what to do with it once you have done it. The problem has vexed us ever since our distant forebears made the welcome discovery that home life could be so much more pleasant if they used the fields instead of the cave for their big jobs.

This momentous turning point in history arrived tens of thousands of years ago. What is so remarkable is how little we progressed until comparatively recent times. The water closet or WC was perfected only within the past 150 years and introduced into the majority of homes during our grandparents' lifetime. Man was walking on the moon and landing spacecraft on Venus by 1970, yet in many parts of this septic isle he still relied on a bucket in a shed or a hole in the ground.

Before we lift the latch to peer into some of those privies and hear what adventures people had with them, let's look back at their long and far from fragrant history.

Two of the oldest known household privies were built at Mohenjo-Daro in India around 2750 BC. The ancient cities of the Indus valley enjoyed water-flushed toilets, and six privies were discovered in the palace of the Sumerian King Sargon, dating from about 2350-2130 BC. Some Ancient Egyptian loos had large, keyhole-shaped holes in their limestone seats, which were carved to accommodate the buttocks. Most astonishing of all, the Minoan Palace of Knossos in Crete boasted an efficient system of water pipes, sewers and latrines, probably with wooden seats and earthenware pans like our modern WCs, with basins alongside to hold water for flushing.

While all this was going on, the Ancient Brits were struggling to build Stonehenge.

The Romans gave us a few ideas after inviting themselves to stay in AD 43. They installed toilet facilities in their larger villas, although it is worth noting that no internal latrines were found in the many posh townhouses excavated at Winchester. In fact, the only Roman loo discovered within the city defences is a chalk-lined pit that may have served the keeper of the South Gate.

At least their Poor Bloody Infantry were properly catered for. The main latrine at Housesteads Fort on Hadrian's Wall seated twenty soldiers at once, ten to a side, on wooden seats above stone troughs flushed with water. At their feet flowed a smaller channel for rinsing out the little sponges on sticks that they used as 'toilet paper' and shared with their comrades. How very pleasant.

Here, as at home, the Romans made their devotions to Crepitus and Stercutius, gods of privies and excrement, and to the sewer-goddess, Venus Cloacina. She is remembered in a heartfelt prayer that people still like to hang on their toilet walls:

> Fayre Cloacina, goddesse of this playce,
> Daylie resorte of all ye human race,
> Grayciouslie grant my offerings may flowe
> Not rudelie swift, nor obstinatelie slowe.

The Middle Ages had hardly begun when the English King Edmund Ironside was killed in the loo by a particularly nasty stab in the back. It was in 1016 that an assassin, 'awaytynge his tyme, espyed when the kynge was at the withdraught to purge nature, and with a spere strake hym into the foundement, and so into the body, whereof kyng Edmunde dyed shortly after'.

Here was an era so steeped in ordure it could be called the Midden Ages. The peasants might simply have obeyed the rule to retire 'a bow's shot away' from dwellings before relieving themselves upon the ground. Sometimes they squatted over holes or pits to store their valuable fertiliser - a practice that survived, virtually unchanged, well into our present century.

The monasteries made sterling efforts to stay out of the muck. Their latrine wings, known as 'reredorters' or 'necessary houses', were often built over a stream, or perhaps the stream might be diverted through a culvert to flush the latrine channel, as at Netley Abbey in southern Hampshire. By 1150, Christchurch Monastery at Canterbury had an elaborate piped water system; the waste and rainwater from the roofs flowed beneath the reredorter, carrying all before it. At St Albans was a necessary 'than which none can be found more beautiful or more sumptuous'. Rainwater stored in a stone cistern flushed it from above, a most unusual arrangement for the times.

The daily rhythm of monastic life meant reredorters had to be big enough to accommodate large numbers of rears at particular times - so many to a sitting, as it were. A row of partitioned seats extended perhaps 160 feet down the length of one wall, and we can picture all those brothers filing silently to their places at the appointed hour, lifting their habits in unison and settling themselves to meditate.

Garderobes, the privies in large medieval houses and castles, were often built into the thick walls on upper floors, with seats of stone or wood from which the excrement went whistling down a shaft or directly into the open air. Sometimes, though, it just slopped out through a chute to slip slowly down the outside wall. Everything landed in a growing heap on the ground, or perhaps in a removable barrel, a huge pit, a stream, or the stagnant moat where fish for the table were conveniently bred. Waste not, want not.

To sit bare-cheeked upon an open-shafted garderobe on a windy winter's day, perhaps suspended precariously in space, must have been a most stimulating experience. An overhanging privy at Chepstow Castle was 200 feet above a river. What a spectacular sight for passers-by when that was in use!

Garderobe chutes and projecting privies can still be seen on the walls of ancient buildings, or you may spot a long external shaft, built to conceal that unsightly brown streak down the wall. Southampton Castle's ingenious garderobes were on at least two storeys of a special tower. Some historians believe they were built on the orders of Henry III - he took a keen interest in all his royal privies. The tower was demolished in the late 19th century but its great sluice or drainage pit, into which everything plummeted, can still be seen near the city walls on Western Esplanade.

What made this set-up so remarkable was a tunnel linking the pit to the foreshore, through which the rising and falling tides

High tides flushed the foreshore beneath these nine garderobe shafts, cut through the Roman wall of Portchester Castle by 12th-century Augustinian monks. This would have been no place to loiter when they were in full flow.

10

automatically washed away the day's accumulations from beneath Henry's fortress - truly a royal flush!

In the crowded towns and cities, laws requiring cesspits to be a certain distance from neighbouring properties were impractical and usually ignored. The Assize of Nuisances dealt with two men who so overfilled their pit that a neighbour found the contents oozing through his wall. Another couple craftily diverted their sewage into next door. 'I only noticed it when my cellar began to overflow,' the outraged recipient told the court.

Equally ingenious was the woman who joined the outlet pipe of her home-made privy to a rainwater gutter. She, too, nearly got away with it but her neighbours complained when the pipe blocked.

The proper people to tackle a brimming privy pit were the 'rakers' or 'gong-fermers'. (Spellings vary: a gong was a privy, and fermer comes from 'to fey', meaning 'to cleanse'.) Their unbelievably dreadful job demanded strong nerve and an even stronger stomach. Often working by night, armed with scoops and buckets, these stalwarts waded - literally - into the massive mounds of malodorous muck. Some of it had festered for a year or more.

Their rewards were deservedly high. In the mid-13th century, thirteen brave men who toiled for five nights to clear the cesspit at Newgate Prison each received sixpence a night, three times the normal rate of pay. A domestic bill from 1450 includes seventeen shillings for 'ye caryyng a way of vj ton of dounge' and five shillings and sixpence for 'dygyng of a pyt and takeyng owte of a serteyne of dounge owte of a privey and for to bery ye dounge in ye same pyt'.

These evil pits (or 'cloaca') could be deep and dangerous. We read of a devout Jew 'which fell into a gong upon the Saturday and would not for reverence of his Sabot day be plucked out;

This typical straight-drop privy in a medieval house has a useful pile of potential manure building beneath it. Such privies often projected directly over the street.

whereof hearing the Earl of Gloucester that the Jew did so great reverence to his Sabot day thought he would do as much unto his holyday, which was Sunday, and so kept him there till Monday, at which season he was foundyn dead'.

Then there was the gong-fermer called Richard the Raker, who in 1326 blithely sat upon his privy, plunged through the rotten boards and drowned 'monstrously in his own excrement'.

Many townhouses had an upstairs, overhanging privy. Everything fell straight through the hole into the street, eventually to be scraped up by a farmer or the official 'scavenger'. Streams and rivers offered tempting alternatives and sometimes house-holders clubbed together to build communal latrines over water or pits.

Public conveniences became increasingly important, as at Winchester, where from the 14th century two great latrines stood strategically near the market and the cathedral. A 'common and long garderobe' extended along the Postern stream; in 1369 a civic-minded citizen called Nicholas Hanyton gave six shillings towards 'roofing, sustaining, mending and maintaining' it. Three years earlier William Inge had been fined, somewhat incongruously, for 'causing a nuisance to the common garderobe' by throwing horse-dung into the Postern stream.

Winchester's other public loo was known as Maydenchamber (possibly from 'midden-chamber'), a long, narrow, timber structure, also built over a stream to carry away the outpourings of its clientele.

The nation's rivers became its sewers. Some of the water-courses in densely populated cities almost ceased to flow, choked with filth. Most of London's rivers were undrinkable from the middle of the 13th century, while the bourn in Sherborne Lane stank so much the locals knew it as Shiteburn Lane.

We can get some idea of medieval practices from this piece of 15th-century advice:

'Beware of draughty privys and of pyssynge in draughts,
and permyt no common pyssyng place about the house
- and let the common house of easement to be over
some water or else elongated from the house.
Beware of emptying pysse pottes and pyssing in chymnes'.

'Draughts' were privies and 'chymnes' were the huge open

fireplaces of the period, temptingly warm places for a quick one when the alternative was a trip to the ice-cold privy.

A ray of hope shone briefly through the muck in 1596 when Sir John Harington, Queen Elizabeth's 'witty godson', invented the water closet and had one working 'in Cloacina's chapel at my house'. Opening a stopper alongside the seat released water from an overhead cistern, flushing the pan's contents into a sluice. Describing it in his *Metamorphosis of Ajax* (the title is a pun on 'a jakes' - a privy), Harington enthused, 'If water be plenty, the oftener it is used, and opened, the sweeter; but if it be scant, once a day is enough, for a need, though twenty persons should use it'. His invention meant that 'your worst privy may be as sweet as your best chamber'.

The idea did not catch on. Although the Queen had one of his WCs installed in her 'Privy-Chamber' at Richmond Palace, with a copy of *Ajax* hanging on a chain beside it, no others are known. Poor old Harington's device was simply a flush in the pan, 200 years ahead of its time.

The aristocracy preferred their comfortable 'stool-rooms'. Each contained a 'close-stool', basically a commode, a large chamber pot inside a wooden box with a padded seat and possibly a lid. Some were fitted with handles to make them portable, others had arms so the user could *really* be enthroned, and many were decorated with velvet, satin, silks, ribbons and ornamental studs.

Presumably, this prettiness did not impress the unfortunate servants who had to empty the foul pots lurking within these whited sepulchres.

Their contents might simply be chucked out into the street, especially after dark. In Scotland, we are told, courtesy demanded a warning shout of 'gardy loo!' (*gardez l'eau*), 'beware of the water!' The frantic response 'hold your hand!' meant 'hang on while I move out of the way - *please!*'

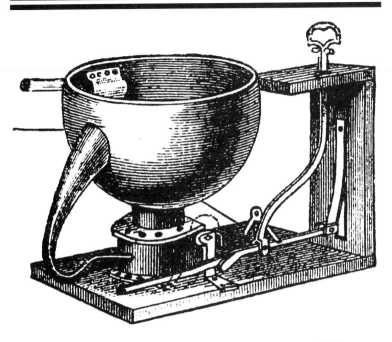

What a Bramah! Joseph Bramah's valve closet was the accepted WC pattern for some 100 years after 1778. The mechanism would have been hidden in a wooden casing.

But the whiff of change was in the air. Rudimentary water closets became viable with the spread of piped water and drains during the 18th century. In 1775 the first patent for a water closet was granted, to Alexander Cummings, a London watchmaker. His S-bend 'stink-trap' overcame the nasty problem of sewer gases seeping back into the house. Only its emptying valve was unreliable, a defect rectified three years later by Joseph Bramah with a WC design that set the standard for more than 100 years. Thousands were sold and the admiring observation 'it's a bramah' came to mean anything of the very best.

While the rich hastened to install the latest WCs, smaller households erected their 'bog houses' or 'Jerichos' over garden cesspits. But the urban poor might share one disgusting privy between twenty or more families and country peasants still used a hole in the ground.

With few public sewers, WCs often flushed into cesspits alongside or actually beneath the houses, soaking into the ground, contaminating wells and releasing foul gases to seep up through the floors. Servants who lived in the basement or kitchen, right above the reeking cesspit, suffered dreadfully. And at emptying time the buckets of filth probably had to be carried through the house by the 'night men', to be dumped in vast communal cesspools or in the nearest river, from which drinking water might still be drawn.

The teeming cities stank. Typhus, typhoid fever, smallpox and diphtheria became commonplace. In 1842, even in the healthiest areas of this country, 28 per cent of children died before reaching the age of five.

The appalling situation in Southampton was described in 1850 by the Public Board of Health's inspector. In one overcrowded slum of 4,378 people he found that 'in some instances the people have no privy accommodation of any kind; in others as many as 44 and 74 persons use a single privy in common. The privies generally are close to the dwellings, the walls in many cases saturated with foetid fluid, and in some instances flowing on to the floors occupied by families.

'In Charlotte Place many filthy privies have not been emptied for 15 years.'

Only after cholera killed tens of thousands around the middle of the century was resolute action taken to improve the nation's water supplies and sewers.

Amazingly, reform was often opposed by vested interests or

ignorant indifference. Proposals to improve the 'appalling state of sanitation' at Bishop's Waltham in Hampshire were rejected repeatedly as 'a waste of money' in the 1830s and again in 1848. As cholera threatened, one villager argued perversely that 'if the existing means of disposal were disturbed, nobody knew what might occur, possibly an epidemic or worse'. And in 1876 plans to replace 'all the old privies and pits' with a modern drainage system were defeated after an influential group persuaded people to turn out and vote against such 'unnecessary and enormous expense'. The village had to wait nearly another 100 years, until 1960, before work began on a proper system of mains sewerage.

Battle lines were drawn up also in Winchester, the 'Drainists' or 'Sewerites' who wanted better sanitation versus the 'Anti-Drainists' or 'Muckabites' - mainly ratepayers who would have to bear the cost. The argument raged for some twenty years.

A special committee in 1849 recommended 'sewering the whole City on a combined and scientific basis' after finding 'one privy amongst two or three families . . . some houses without any privy or outlet of any description . . . open and offensive ditches, drains, gutters, gratings and other outlets, constantly emitting noxious effluvia and contaminating both the air and water which the inhabitants are under the necessity of using'.

And yet at numerous public meetings, despite deaths from cholera, the Muckabites won the day and Winchester continued to stink. This foolish song demonstrated their complacency:

The Muckabites' Triumph
Good health to all the Muckabites,
Heigh ho! Stink O!
Who love to have their Dirty nights,
Heigh ho! Stink O!
Our Cesspools shall not be Drained,

Heigh ho! Stink O!
Our Slush-holes shall be retained,
Heigh ho! Stink O!
As for Fevers, we don't fear,
Heigh ho! Stink O!
So long as we can get strong beer,
Heigh ho! Stink O!
Nor yet for Cholera do we care,
Heigh ho! Stink O!
So it's goodbye to all ye Sewerites,
Heigh ho! Stink O!
We mean to die firm Muckabites,
Heigh ho! Stink O!

The late-19th century saw WCs come out of the closet, liberated from their wooden surrounds to become magnificent glazed thrones in a variety of richly decorated shapes, with deservedly splendid names: Sultan, Aquarius, Waterfall, Deluge, Cascade,

Two magnificent thrones. Doulton's 'Lambeth' and the 'Lion' by Edward Johns, surely the most astonishing of all the ornamental Victorian WC bowls.

Ripple, Lambeth, Excelsior, Dolphin, Westminster Portcullis, Rocket, Perfecta, Clencher, Alerto . . . the list was endless.

Some of them bore makers' names familiar today, like John Shanks, Henry Doulton and Thomas Twyford, creator of the first WC made all in earthenware. There was also Thomas Crapper, who many people believe gave us our WC and the word 'crap'. He did neither. 'Crap' had been around for some 700 years before old Tom contributed to its disposal by inventing his Valveless Water-Waste Preventer, a mechanism to save water by delivering a measured amount and no more until the cistern refilled. Look inside your toilet cistern. That's what Crapper perfected.

Before mains water reached World's End, this 1930s privy on Harold Nobes' farm - right alongside the main road - was flushed by rainwater which was collected from the farmhouse roof into two huge, elevated tanks and piped across by gravity into the WC cistern.

It was to be a very long time before all the privies perished. Many local councils - the major builders of rural housing after 1918 - were still not providing bathrooms or WCs in new houses in the late 1930s, neither was mains sewerage installed in some villages until many years after that.

As the 20th century completed its sixth decade, Hampshire folk were still scurrying down the garden path to the privy.

[2]

First Choose Your Privy

One of the first people I met when I began prying into privies was born in Cheriton during the Second World War. He remembers watching his father dig down into their back garden until he reached water, which was never far below the surface, before dragging into position over the soggy hole a rusty tin shack containing a wooden seat. The family privy was back in business! When they'd filled the hole, Dad simply dug another. And another.

It went on for years. Nobody seemed to mind, least of all the watercress growers whose beds bordered the garden. 'It was really marvellous cress,' my new friend assured me.

Crude bog houses like that were used for hundreds of years. All it took was a hole or pit beneath some form of seat, perhaps just a wooden plank or bough, with a screen or hut to make things private. The liquid waste could usually be relied upon to seep away into the earth, while over the weeks the good stuff piled up into a usable load for digging out as fertiliser for the garden. Or the hole might simply be filled in and a new one prepared. In a well-ordered pit privy, layers of earth or ashes helped to kill the smell and keep the flies away.

Bad drainage was bad news. A pit half full of watery sewage was not a pretty sight, while the rotten job of emptying it was made doubly difficult.

One popular solution was to build a 'dry' or 'vault' privy. The pit (or 'vault') had a solid base inclining gently backwards to drain any water into the garden through a small brick archway at the back of the privy. A pile of earth against the archway prevented the solid waste from escaping. The best vaults, those that

21

could most easily be emptied and cleaned, had walls and floor of concrete or brick.

A champion of the dry privy claimed in 1896, somewhat optimistically, that it 'requires no looking after and is never offensive; all that it requires is that it should be emptied once every six months or so, and this is done without trouble in five minutes, when the earth and the droppings are shovelled out on the level and mixed with a little more earth, after which a barrow full of fresh earth is tipped against the archway, and that is all that is wanted. If what has been taken out is left in a heap for two or three weeks it becomes valuable manure for the garden.'

Dry privies were still being used until quite recently. Irene Cranston of Ewshot remembers her neighbours putting theirs to good use. 'Into the large hole at the back went also leaves and weeds, all the waste, human and otherwise, to be used in their garden. I guess it was a compost heap! Luckily our cottage was some way off, for at times, especially in hot weather, it didn't exactly smell of violets.'

Mr Penney of Colbury directed me to the sad remains of one which had been built onto the end of a farm shed. All was crumbling and overgrown with brambles but enough was left to identify the wooden boxed seat and the pit round the back.

'I used to help my father empty that old dunnekin, always on a moonlit night,' Mr Penney told me. 'We would put on our rubber boots, shovel it out into the family tin bath and dump it on the manure heap with the cow muck. Then it all got spread on the fields.'

Other folk much preferred to get someone else to do the shovelling, particularly when the contents had piled up for months. In the early 1920s, Mr Hunt from Downton, near Lymington, lived in a row of four cottages at Pennington, where the outdoor privies consisted of two large vaults, each one shared between two houses. 'The vaults were used until full - about a year's use.

When they had to be emptied, two old men were paid one pound each to do the job at night. All the cottage windows were sealed on these occasions, as the contents had to be ladled out into an old garden watering tub on iron wheels. This was then drawn up through the village and tipped on the allotments known as Pound Ground, where the council estate is now built.

'It was just spread on the surface and allowed to dry, after which it was dug into the ground. Some of this material was no more than 30 yards away from a house at the end of one terrace - not very hygienic!

'The one pound each paid to the two men was for emptying one vault. This seems a very small sum today but at that time it was nearly a week's wages to some people.'

I think most people would demand considerably more than that for tackling even a month's accumulations from two families, let alone a full year's!

The vault privy at Manor Farm in the country park at Bursledon, near Southampton, is an impressive three-holer, complete with rear archway for drainage and emptying. And, as was the custom, one of its holes is smaller than the others, just right for a child's bum.

In the world of privies, the most sanitary convenience seems to have been the earth closet. Its praises were sung by many hygienists who favoured it over the vault or the simple bucket. What appealed to them was that after each performance the 'faecal matter' (a wonderful euphemism!) could be covered with a layer of dry earth, delivered into the bucket from a hopper at the back of the closet. The aforesaid faecal matter was instantly deodorised and, it was claimed, quickly became sterile, ideal for digging into the garden plot.

Like a dry privy, the best results came from excluding as much water as possible. Gentlemen and boys who just needed to stand

The privy at Manor Farm in the country park at Bursledon is believed to date from about 1900.

Three-hole seats were quite common and even six-holers are not unknown. There was usually a smaller hole for children, as here at Manor Farm.

were often expected to go behind a bush rather than use the bucket.

Obtaining regular supplies of clean, fine, very dry earth could be a bind. Some people remember having to dry garden earth in the household oven, in front of the fire, or in the little stoves sold especially for the purpose, like a small furnace beneath a metal tray.

Charcoal or ashes from the fire were considered poor alternatives. One Medical Officer of Health advised that 'the effect of dry earth upon excreta is very different from that of ashes, for it is found that it serves to make the excreta not only inoffensive but to effect complete change in [them], so that their original character cannot be recognised, and even if paper be mixed with them this disappears at the same time.'

The Reverend Henry Moule of Fordington, near Dorchester,

MOULE'S EARTH CLOSETS

Apparatus on Bearers ready to Fix.
Deal Seat 3' 0" Long.
No. A1724. " Pull Out," as drawn.
No. A1725. " Pull Up " Pattern.
No. A1726. " Self-acting " Pattern.

Strong, Portable, Self-Contained Set. Plain Deal. Galvanized Fittings. Pail complete. 21" Wide. 27" Back to Front.

No. A1727. " Pull Out." (as drawn)
No. A1728. " Pull Up "

Strong, Portable, Self-contained.
Best Plain Deal.
Fittings of Galvanized Iron.
With Pail complete.
No. A1729. Self-Acting. 21" Wide.
27" Back to Front. 36" High.

No.		
A1724	.. ..	**57/6**
A1725	.. ..	**70/-**
A1726	.. ..	**100/-**
*A1727	.. ..	**72/6**
*A1728	.. ..	**86/6**
*A1729	.. ..	**102/6**

* Pails included.
Other Pails **3/7** Each Extra.

First patented in 1860, the Rev Henry Moule's earth closets were still popular at the outbreak of World War II. This ironmonger's catalogue of 1936 includes the automatic or 'self-acting' model (bottom).

The earth closet with its boarding removed to show how pulling the handle swung the metal hopper forwards, chucking a measure of earth or ashes into the bucket.

patented the earth closet in 1860, later designing a portable model ('invaluable in sick rooms, in hospitals and in infirmaries') and an ingenious self-acting one which delivered the earth automatically when the user arose from the throne. It cost five pounds, two shillings and sixpence in 1936, 'in Best Plain Deal, pail included'. Many companies took out licences to make 'Moules' and they sold in thousands, all over the world, to be installed in homes, factories, schools, barracks and prisons. Wakefield Gaol had 776. I have seen them offered for sale in ironmongery catalogues from William Dibben of Southampton as late as 1939.

In some Moules, the earth was chucked into the bucket when a side handle was pulled up. Others had a little pull-out handle attached directly to the swinging hopper, and this was the sort

27

Dave Robinson shows me how the old earth closet looked when he found it. The hinged lid is in place above the hopper, which was boarded in.

found by Dave Robinson of Alton. Dave, a stonemason, was allowed to rescue the turn-of-the-century closet from a derelict office formerly used by the sexton in a local cemetery. I donated it on his behalf to the Hampshire Buildings Preservation Trust, who hope to conserve this important relic at their Bursledon Brickworks site. After all, the privy is as much a part of our social history as any other building.

Some homes had pits, others had earth closets. The majority relied upon The Bucket, despite this stern warning in a textbook on sanitary engineering from 1925: 'Given a suitable situation approached from the external air and adequate attention, earth-closets can be maintained in a condition free from nuisance; but the same cannot be said of a [bucket] privy, for, regarded sanitarily, it is practically impossible to avoid nui-

The best bucket privies had a lid to reduce the nuisance from flies. This rather neglected specimen also has a splash guard and a front access door for emptying.

sance, even if the greatest care is exercised. This being so, their use can only be justified in circumstances where an earth-closet is unworkable'.

Folk were not put off by such defeatist talk. The beauty of the bucket was its simplicity. There were no moving parts to go wrong, no huge piles of unpleasantness to be shovelled out periodically and no great expense in setting up your privy. All you needed was a seat over a bucket, preferably a nice big one, somewhere to house it and some means of emptying it.

'Bucket and chuck it' was the motto. You could bury 'it' in your garden and watch the vegetables flourish, allow a convenient river to whisk away your problem, or wait for the nice men from the council to come round with their cart.

Mr Clarke from Millbrook in Southampton grew up in the city's Waterside area, in 'the days of no mains drainage or cesspits in the garden. Our outside loo, all we had of course, adjoined the garden shed. Gran always called it the Dubb House. It was not very big, just big enough. A wooden frame, a corrugated iron roof and whitewashed walls. The loo was a deep pot under a wooden seat with a fairly large hole in it. As you can imagine, as the excrement got higher in the pot it wasn't a lot of fun or very hygienic.

'As you sat there, gathering your thoughts, you often felt the cold wind in winter coming through the gap at the bottom of the loo and up around your rear end. Not much fun.

'Dad would have his fag out there, and of course the time would come when one would have to say, "Dad, could you empty the loo bucket?" That was done at the bottom of the garden, where the rhubarb was growing.'

Families often had to share the privy with others, especially in the towns. At Romsey, in what is now called King John's Garden but was formerly Church Court, an unusual communal

Behind the restored communal privies of Church Court, Romsey. Flowing upwards in this picture, the stream was directed under five open seats by the cleverly curved brickwork, flushing out the falling waste of perhaps eight families.

privy block stood on brick piers over the river, into which everything fell directly.

Betty Russell, whose mother raised nine children in Church Court, remembers it still being used in 1939, possibly serving eight families. Newspaper squares hung on nails by wooden box seats in the whitewashed cubicles. Women had the first one, a single-holer, and also the middle cubicle, which housed an adults' hole next to a lower seat for children. In the third, two men could sit side by side, discussing world affairs as the river flushed conveniently beneath, just inches from their backsides.

'Mother used to send us to the Town Hall with a bottle on Sunday mornings,' Betty told me. 'A man at the side entrance filled it with a thick, black disinfectant, and mother would dilute a drop in a bucket of water to scrub the seats. I suppose the other women took their turn. The privy always smelled clean and fresh.

'If it rained we children used to play in there. We played in the river, too - always upstream, of course!'

[3]

Down The Garden Path

'Why don't you use its proper name?' wrote a rather cross gentleman. 'It is not a privy, a toilet or a loo. It is a lavatory.'

Well, there probably never was a 'proper name', but privy and loo can claim pedigrees hundreds of years long. Privy derives from the Old French *privé*, meaning private, and loo probably comes from *lieu d'aisance*, which translates wonderfully as 'place of comfort' or 'easing place'. People would ask for the *lieu*, the place, wrongly pronouncing it as 'loo'.

Lavatory and toilet are more modern euphemisms, recently adopted to avoid mentioning the unmentionable. Both originally were to do with washing, rather than relieving, oneself, and ironmongers' catalogues from the turn of the century confirm that lavatories were *wash basins*, not WCs. 'Going to my toilet' or 'using the lavatory' became convenient alternatives to the equally coy 'wash my hands'. Now, thanks to the peculiar way our language develops, the definitions of lavatory and toilet have altered entirely.

My grumpy correspondent also demanded to know why I thought anyone could possibly be interested in 'such a distasteful subject'. Perhaps the answer lies in this letter, written in a neat, careful hand on small squares of notepaper and sent with no address other than 'New Forest area'. The writer is clearly someone who appreciated the romance, the charm and delight of the British privy.

'I lived for two years with relatives in a New Forest village. The privy was like a little house, built of brick with a red-tiled roof. It was a sanctuary to which members of the family sometimes went for a bit of peace and quiet. The lid of the well-scrubbed cabinet could be pulled down, making a good seat for a child. Adults would sit on a side part. When paying a visit one could hear birds on the roof or the pattering of rain. Often the door was left half open and I remember a gravel path outside, fragrant with lilacs and other shrubs, and the sound of hens. The door had an iron latch, which was stubborn at times. This was frightening for children, who thought they would be trapped for a long time. Oh, the bliss when the latch was lifted!'

Plenty of other letters contained similar sentiments, like these from S. Harfield: 'My grandparents' privy was a place for contemplation and escape, somewhere to muse awhile and kick little feet against the solid backboards. It was cool and quiet and never smelt. There was a wonderful keyhole view of the garden through a knothole in the back. I loved that privy.'

Denise Evans sent happy memories of her grandparents' privy, 'discreetly situated down the garden path' at their bungalow on the Hampshire/Surrey border. 'As a child I remember sitting on the wooden seat with the door open and being able to see across the garden and over the hedge into the field beyond. The newspaper squares on the spike were there to be examined, and the bucket under the seat was a source of interest - how did it come out?

'My grandmother was very conscious of hygiene but although this extended to the privy, nothing could mask that unmistakable odour. I remember I was expected to only "spend a penny" on my weekly visits to them.'

Sandra Naish of Bitterne told me that her grandfather's brick-built 'bucket and chuck it' at Crampmoor 'smelt quite sweet, as he was fastidious about his loo. There was a shovel and a container of sawdust, which I was taught to sprinkle into the bucket to cover things after use. This was a fine game for a town child in a different environment.'

I came across this little beauty by accident, down the path in a gloriously unkempt Botley garden.

Mrs Hayward of Bitterne remembers how 'in the winter, mother used to put a lighted candle on a saucer, cover it with an earthenware flower pot and put it in the lavatory to keep it warm.'

'My grandparents had two privies at their big, rented house in Warsash,' says Mrs Jones. 'Grandma took in lodgers, people who came to sail on the boats under the auspices of Graham White and later Lord Stawbridge. One privy, made of wood and varnished every year, was for ladies and children. It backed on to a tool shed at the front of the building. There were two holes, one large, the other smaller with a step-up box for children. Grandad used to take the buckets from the tool shed side, the back, so that no guests should witness the operation.

'A bit further along the path and well hidden by a bay tree and a may tree was a stone building for the men. It was whitewashed inside and out once a year. I was never allowed to even go round by the door of this place.'

I doubt whether today's generation will speak so lovingly of their shiny, comfortable, *unadventurous* bathrooms. You never knew what you would find on that journey down the path, nor what lay behind the latched door. Often it didn't even lock so you had to sing to let others know you were there, or perhaps you would sing from the sheer joy of the occasion.

But if you were a small person in a big, dark, spooky privy, you sometimes sang to keep your spirits up.

Paul Humber of Cupernham had to brave the winter gales in his family's terrifying two-holer beneath an old elm tree. 'The privy swayed about in strong winds because the tree roots underneath were loose. We used to fear the tree coming down with us in there, the door would fly open, wind and rain came in at the open back where dad pulled the bucket out - one did not hang around in this place.

Beneath the trees - friendly enough in the sunlight, but imagine paying a visit out here after dark, the eerie silence broken only by strange rustlings in the undergrowth!

'My brother said there was a bogey man down there, so at night I took a lantern and ran there and back, mindful of the wind moving the bog to and fro. It was an eerie experience for a six year old. Later on I would just tiddle in the grass half way down.'

The family bucket privy at Stoke Common that Jean Kingdon used was, like many others, joined to and reached through the shed for wood, coal and tools. Shed and privy were corrugated iron, 'covered with rambling roses, the old-fashioned moss rose and two others, one red and one pink. An apple tree overhung it. You can imagine what it was like, especially after dark, to hear twigs scratching the corrugated iron, or maybe an apple suddenly falling on the metal roof.'

Jean Treble's parents raised seven children in an old thatched cottage near Hannington, with a one-hole privy in a windowless

Straight down the garden path - you can't miss it! 'Semi-detached' privies at Durley.

Ronald Hansford of Hardley still sometimes uses the bucket privy built by his grandfather in 1923. For many years their only lavatory, it lies deep inside the former pig shed. Grandfather erected old gates and hurdles to guide his pigs into the truck on market days, obliging the family to clamber frantically over them should they need to 'go'.

hut down the end of the path. 'Newspaper was torn into squares and threaded with binder twine,' says Jean. 'In winter we were allowed to use a candle but more often than not the wind blew it out and you would imagine all sorts of spooky things and run faster than lightning in case the bogey man caught you.

'In summertime, Mum would put glow-worms in a jam jar. We used to think it great fun, and the wind could not blow them out.'

Joan Whitley of Hedge End was born in a house facing Botley Square, on the corner just above Botley Mill. 'The privy was at the bottom of the garden, very close to the mill. It had a wooden seat over a hole which went I know not where. I was always terrified of falling down it and never getting out. Sometimes you could hear the water from the river splashing. My grandparents,

Meet your neighbours. An assortment of doors on four privies at Titchfield, one each for the terraced cottages behind them. They hold flush toilets now, some still in daily use.

Rupert Gillett hopes to restore the ancient family privy at West End. He was one of five children who had to dash 20 yards from their house. A laurel bush screened it from the neighbours and the tin bath (right) hung on the side until Friday bath night.

41

whose home it was, assured me it was when the tide came in.'

Denise Graham often stayed with her aunt at Hambledon, where the privy was in a woodshed at the end of the garden path, surrounded by stinging nettles in the summer. 'We used to take a candle in a jam jar and if it was windy it went out, leaving you groping in the dark for the squares of newspaper on the nail behind the door. Oh, what memories!'

Mabel Evans of Hythe recalls a common complaint of older brothers and sisters. 'Why did my younger sister always seem to need it on nights that were dark! That meant a candle in a jam jar, up a nettle-lined path, spiders to be removed from the seat (my job) and then the wait.'

As a child and living with her grandparents, Daphne Kingsland of Wickham 'was allowed, usually once a year, to whitewash the inner wooden walls of the privy. One year, I remember, the only colour wash available was a sickly green. Crossing the yard on winter evenings, I guarded the flame of a flickering candle and felt terrified on entering the dark shed, certain that someone or something was lurking in the shadows.'

Sometimes the dangers were real, not just imagined. Sheila Petty of West End remembers visits to her parents' friends, whose privy was under large laurel hedges. She was about ten at the time. 'It always seemed to be my responsibility to take my younger sister when she wanted to use it. I didn't mind this, but what I did mind was that chickens roosted in the hedge or on the roof and, not enjoying being disturbed, would squawk and fly down in front of us, frightening us out of our wits. If we needed to use it in the dark I used to take a broom with me for protection.'

Grace Taylor of Aldershot had an uncomfortable encounter with a three-hole privy while visiting her grandparents. Just four years old, she was bravely performing alone among fat

A little privy at Romsey, recently restored, which conveniently backed onto a stream.

brown spiders and dusty cobwebs when the door blew shut, plunging her into darkness.

'I finished what I went in to do, then climbed onto the seat, reaching about for a chain to pull, as I would have done at home. In the dark I fell through one of the holes, plunging straight into the gruesome mess in the big bucket. Someone heard me screaming, yanked me out and promptly immersed me in a wooden barrel full of cold water, still fully clothed except for my lost knickers. Then I was scrubbed down with carbolic soap. I still shudder to remember it.'

Sue Wallace recalls the obstacle her husband always faced on childhood visits to his aunt and uncle at Hursley. Their two sheepdogs, Rover and Toby, had kennels either side of the garden path leading to the privy. Six-year-old Robert's troubles began the day he mischievously puffed air from a bellows into

This square-shaped building at Botley served two cottages. One door was your privy, the other your fuel shed. What a pity a modern door mars an otherwise attractive relic.

Rover's face as the dog snoozed in front of the fire. 'Rover never forgot,' says Sue. 'Many years later young Robert was still running the gauntlet between the two kennels, with Rover at the length of his chain, trying to reach the boy who had treated him so badly.'

It wasn't only the young who feared that gloomy path. Miss Halfacre of Eastleigh recalls a cold winter's night when, scared stiff after a family session of ghost stories, she had to ask her boyfriend to accompany her down the eerily quiet garden to a relative's privy. 'It was the spookiest of places in the dark and best avoided at all costs. I told him to wait outside and not dare move. All the time I was in the privy I kept asking if he was still there. Mission accomplished, out I came, only to be told that he

44

Four picturesque privies of considerable vintage (one with its door missing),
way down the garden paths behind terraced cottages in Catisfield. You could
certainly keep an eye on your neighbours' comings and goings with this
arrangement!

needed to use the loo now. So I found myself outside in the dark,
hanging on to the door latch, absolutely petrified.'

Denis Padwick, too, was sometimes called upon to lend a com-
forting hand. 'Near our house were tall elm trees, home to a
colony of screech owls, whose loud noises were heard all evening
during the winter. We kids were in no way scared of them, but
after darkness fell we did proceed down the garden slowly, hand
carefully cupped round a cheerful candle flame.

'Mum was a bit nervous sometimes because of possible drunks
straying up the passage and so I was deputed as her escort,
standing a comfortable five yards or so away until she was
ready to return.'

[4]

DON'T FORGET THE PAPERWORK

Most folk made do with squares of newspaper in their privy and thought nothing of it, well into the second half of the 20th century. They were recycling paper long before the practice became fashionable. 'But didn't the print come off?' I hear some young people cry. Of course it did, much worse than from today's papers, but it washed off easily enough on bath night. Having an inky bum was no disgrace.

Posh alternatives for those who sought pristine buttocks included brown wrapping paper and glossy magazines, notably *Picture Post*, although the glossies did present their own problems. Not to put too fine a point on it, shiny paper tended to spread rather than remove. It was reputed also to play havoc with the haemorrhoids.

Much nicer was soft paper, like the small squares once used to wrap tangerines, apples and other fruit. These scraps were jealously hoarded to provide an occasional, blissful treat. But even this simple pleasure could be hazardous, as some wrappers were printed with cheap, garish pigments which dissolved when damp, startling the unwary who discovered multi-coloured streaks on their cheeks.

A lady in Upham confided, almost guiltily, 'We never used newspaper in our privy, only tissue paper. Perhaps we were better off. Mum used to save it, or perhaps she bought it. My sister and I would cut it up into squares and put string through the corners.'

This chore of making the squares, whether of tissue or newspaper, seems to have been delegated to the young in most families. Older children used metal meat skewers to pierce holes for the string by which the sheaf would hang on a nail in the privy. The art lay in gauging how many sheets could safely be perforated at once before the skewer suddenly burst through, out of control, to puncture little fingers.

Many people recalled happy memories of privy paper. Here's Brenda Kerslake, speaking of her childhood in Portsmouth. 'Our toilet was outside the back door. It was my job to make squares of newspaper and my father put the hole in and threaded the string through. Then when the oranges and apples came in, with tissue paper round, we used that instead.'

Neither was Mabel Evans of Hythe alone in identifying a common annoyance. 'On Saturdays the newspaper was cut into neat squares and a hole made with a meat skewer for the string, but how very frustrating when having a quiet read out there to find the end of the story missing!'

Even the aristocracy sometimes had mucky buttocks. Prince Albert was notorious for introducing stringent economies in the royal residences. So insistent was Queen Victoria that nothing should change after Albert's death in 1861 (from typhoid, let it be noted) that 31 years later an equerry could still write peevishly from Windsor Castle, 'We all admire various little economical thrifty dodges here. In the WCs - NEWSPAPER squares.' One courtier, he added, had suggested sending the lot, post unpaid, to the Master of the Queen's Household by way of protest.

We are told that sensitive Victorian ladies couldn't bring themselves to mention toilet paper. They looked the shopkeeper straight in the eye and ordered 'a packet of curl papers'. He knew what was meant. Perhaps it was handed over in a plain brown wrapper . . .

Victoria herself is said to have had her sensibilities respected when visiting Cambridge. Crossing the Cam, which like many

47

rivers in those days was little more than a common sewer, she asked, 'What are all those pieces of paper floating down the

The editions featuring portraits of Hitler were particularly popular . . .

river?' Quick as a flash, the Master of Trinity College assured her, 'Those, ma'am, are notices that bathing is forbidden.'

All manner of reading material has met its fate in the privy. Joyce Stevens from Headley tells me that 'we were able to obtain a thick Army and Navy Stores catalogue, with its hundreds of thin papers, which lasted a long time. It made interesting reading, too.'

Trashy literature, newspapers and pamphlets were called 'bum-fodder' as far back as the 17th century, and tiresome paperwork is still known as 'bumf'. A satirical verse from 1660, about the Rump Parliament, bears the title *Bumm-Fodder; or, Waste-Paper proper to wipe the nation's rump with, or your own*, and published in 1753 was *Bum-Fodder for the Ladies; a Poem (Upon Soft Paper)*.

The ready availability of printed matter during those private moments when there was little else to occupy the brain did at least encourage the sitter to read, if only from curiosity or boredom. Newspaper extracts plucked at random from the nail introduced new worlds to youngsters who otherwise might never read anything more profound than a comic paper. They opened their minds as they opened their bowels and so were doubly enriched by the experience.

Purpose-made toilet paper came first in ready cut blocks (some makers proudly offered their squares 'Ready Stringed'), then in continuous rolls and finally as the perforated roll we buy today. The latter seems to have emerged in the 1880s. Its makers included the Scott brothers in Philadelphia, who went on to become a household name, and over here the British Patent Perforated Paper Company.

Millions of former sufferers will remember the BPPPC for its notorious glazed paper, 'Bronco'. Just as we British believed that such insanities as cold baths, boarding schools and flogging were character building, so we stoically endured Bronco, Izal and similar papers whose composition was so unsuited to their intended purpose. Hard, shiny, unloved yet perversely prevalent, they skidded across the nation's backsides for generations.

This was probably the stuff enjoyed by Mrs M.R. Jones from North Baddesley while growing up in the waterside village of Warsash during the 1920s and '30s. 'We had the luxury of toilet paper that came off the liners,' she remembers. 'There were always packs to be picked up off the shore between Warsash and Hook. This was dried slowly in the oven and I spent many hours pulling string through one corner to hang it up by.'

In a trade catalogue of 1905, I found offered for sale packets of paper containing 500 sheets 'wired for hanging up'. There was also The Tonbar, a toilet roll holder 'in brass, with match holder and tray for spent matches'. The Sanitary Paper Company advertised a holder for 'special rolls of toilet paper which is 500 ft long and is not perforated, as any length from an inch upwards can be instantly detached by means of the patent cutter'. No suggestion was made as to who might wish to manage with a one-inch piece of toilet paper.

Another manufacturer listed a bewildering range of papers:

Special Line (the cheapest, 2s. 3d per doz.)
Medium Quality
Better Quality
Thick
Thick, Non-Perforated
Glazed Manilla
Thin Manilla, Unglazed
Medicated Terebene
Medicated Terebene, Super (the dearest, 11s. 3d per doz).

They reminded me of the spoof advert we passed around at school: 'Try Tinker's Textured Toilet Paper. It comes in four grades - thin, very thin, extremely thin and UUGH!!'

When next you reach for a soft sheet of toilet tissue, pause and remember the privy pioneers. In former times, or when paper wasn't available, folk had to manage with what came to hand. Hay, straw, wool, herbs, feathers and leaves are all recorded as having served the needy, and there's probably a lot of truth in the verse traditionally chanted in Hampshire playgrounds:

> In days of old when knights were bold
> And paper weren't invented,
> They wiped their arse on tufts of grass
> And went away contented.

The Romans liked to cleanse themselves with perfumed wool. They also used sponges tied to sticks, which in communal latrines were rinsed after use and left in containers of brine for the next lucky customer. Cloths or rags have been favoured over the centuries, sometimes being laundered for reuse, while the excavated privy pits of monasteries have revealed that the monks made good use of the torn-up remnants of their old habits. Tears spring to the eyes at the thought of employing pine-cones, stones or curved sticks, yet all were commonly used at various times in history.

Consider finally this charming example of privy etiquette, described in 1751 by Samuel Rolleston in his *Philosophical Dialogue Concerning Decency*:

> 'Our Ladies in England are asham'd of being seen even in going to or returning from the most necessary parts of our houses, as if it was in itself shameful to do even in private what nature absolutely requires at certain seasons to be done; whereas I have known an old woman in Holland set herself on the next hole to a Gentleman, and civilly offer him her mussel shell by way of scraper after she had done with it herself.'

[5]

NATURE'S BOUNTY

Shivering in a dark and draughty privy on a bitter winter's night with only your guttering candle for comfort was no fun, but at least you had the grim satisfaction of knowing your labours would bear fruit - provided, of course, you had the good sense to obey Nature's law by recycling her bounty. Those who dutifully performed the burial ceremony were assured of garden produce the size and taste of which has never been surpassed.

These wooden privies behind terraced cottages at Southwick were in use until 1970. Each shed was divided into two single-holers, one each for neighbouring cottages, their doors facing the bottom of the gardens. 'Before council collections began in 1955, Dad emptied the bucket on the compost heap for his garden and allotment,' said a resident.

Consider the testimony of Mrs Jones of North Baddesley, who told me how her grandfather 'buried all the contents of the privy bucket deep in the garden, left it for ages, and later crops were grown over it - the best raspberries and gooseberries I have ever eaten.'

Or this from Denis Padwick, about the occasion when his mother was away for medical treatment. 'My dad and elder brothers took advantage of the opportunity to make a trench and empty our bucket into it, along with the neighbours' productions, covering the noisome contents with earth and planting the runner beans. Mum, returning very much better in health, was amazed at the quantity and quality of that year's crop. I don't think Dad revealed the secret until after the beans had all been eaten.

'My brother-in-law similarly buried the "waste" in his garden at Hartley Wespall. Newly married and previously no gardener, he wondered at first why magnificent tomatoes grew where none had been planted. He soon cottoned on.'

Meanwhile, Mrs Downes's father 'used to empty the bucket in the garden every Friday night, then shake carbolic powder in the bucket. I must say we had a lovely garden of vegetables and flowers. When I was about ten years old, my job on Saturday morning was to scrub the wooden seat and whiten the cement floor before putting a clean sack on it. I was not allowed out to play until I did these chores.'

Mrs Crosswell and her husband discovered that a huge mound of ashes in the back garden of their newly rented cottage at Waltham Chase was the repository for not only the kitchen waste but also the products of a big privy bucket. 'My husband eventually managed to level the garden, spreading all the ashes over the ground, which was mostly clay. It did wonders for the soil and we grew most everything.'

The corrugated iron 'bucket and chuck it' privy, now at Manor Farm, which formerly served at least three people in a Longparish family.

Sometime around 1950, their council 'honeycart' began collecting the buckets. 'I believe it was emptied at a market garden and ploughed in,' says Mrs Crosswell. 'One particular day the doctor arrived just as the council man was carrying out our bucket. The doctor was amazed and said, "Surely you aren't letting them take that away, are you?" He said he was a firm believer in digging it into the earth.'

Even the wild spots flourished. Mabel Evans of Hythe recalls her father ritually lighting his pipe and calling 'Any more for the portmanteau?' - his name for the huge family bucket - before struggling off into the nearby wood. 'Spring meant wood anemones, celandines, bluebells and even my mum's forget-me-nots in profusion,' says Mabel. 'Chelsea Flower Show? No, nature at her very best in our wood.'

Two paces out the back door and up the step. This half wood, half brick privy in a garden at Brook couldn't be more convenient.

'Semi-detached' privies at Botley, converted into garden sheds.

Second hand from Sue Wallace comes her husband's memory of when he was eight and his sister eleven years old. Their Saturday job was to dispose of the week's supply from the family loo in Hedge End. 'They used to carry the bucket to the end of the garden and dig a hole. Many's the time the cry went up, "Oh no, we dug here last week! Fill it in again!" He reckons they had the best strawberries in the district, though.'

David Gentle outlined the finer points with his memories of the bucket at North Baddesley, where he lived for some twenty years before 1961. 'We were supposed to have a rota for emptying it. Sod's Law ensured it was always my turn when the bucket was overflowing and I had on my best Teddy Boy suit, going out for rock and roll.

'The method was: (i) dig your hole; (ii) lift out bucket, simultaneously holding your breath; (iii) hold bucket as far away from

It proved impossible to get into this tantalisingly overgrown privy at Horton Heath. 'I cannot even remember what's in there,' said the owner. I left, frustrated and still curious.

clothes as possible; (iv) run like the Devil, trying not to trip with your dangerous cargo; (v) deposit contents into hole in one quick tip; (vi) backfill hole and replace bucket.

'Sometimes we would dig a complete trench and refill it gradually over the weeks. Some trenches were not very deep and it was a recognised hazard that you might sink up to your ankles in forgotten earthworks. We always discovered tomatoes aplenty growing over earlier sites.'

Some canny folk even made a few bob from what had cost them nothing but a bit of effort. There was no bucket in the privy when Barbara Johnston of Millbrook was a child, just a seat hole with nothing beneath. 'When it was full, Dad opened a door in the outside wall and with a long-handled shovel emptied it into a hole under the rhubarb, which grew very well indeed.

We didn't eat the rhubarb, but sent it to market.'

More rhubarb, this time from Miss Halfacre. As a child, she loved visiting the privy at a relative's cottage near Hursley. 'Just behind the latched door was a large container of ashes and a small shovel. Sprinkling ashes into a bucket instead of pulling on a chain was absolutely fascinating!

'Their garden produce thrived and the rhubarb grew like small trees. It wasn't until I grew up that I realised the secret of their delicious rhubarb tarts.'

Iris Gover from Longdown, who told me so many lovely stories, recalls how 'my friend Hilda fell out with her husband Albert. He always refused to empty the bucket after her big family came for weekends. They were pubbers, Albert was not, and the bucket smelled of beer. Poor Hilda had to get up early to empty it herself. She said it was her nightmare.'

[6]

'The Honeycart's Coming!'

Some people simply could not face a ripe privy pail or pit, and who shall blame them? Others, having no gardens, couldn't empty theirs even had they wished. But the job had to be done, which is where a magnificent breed of men came into their own. With nerves of iron and stomachs of steel, these heroic successors to the medieval gong-fermers vigorously tackled the privies of a grateful nation.

Often employed or contracted by the council, they usually arrived after dark to collect the 'night soil' in the 'night cart', affectionately known as the honeycart, honeywagon, lavender cart, Stink-bomb Tommy, dunnekin-drag, Bombay mail cart, violet cart, perfumery - the list was limited only by the imagination.

In Romsey during the 1920s, says Denis Padwick, 'buckets were removed once or twice a week and replaced by reasonably clean ones, pretty quietly I may say, by The Romsey Night Chariot, a large, four-wheeled, horse-drawn cart. Each afternoon it was driven through the town, laden with empty buckets, and parked in the council yard until collection started, around midnight.

'It was based at Budds Lane, off Greatbridge Road, where the buckets were emptied into lakes of effluent and covered with ash - plentifully available from weekly collections of the residue of hundreds of open fires. We boys knew this establishment as The Shitty. One day a friend of mine fell into one of the lakes, becoming *persona non grata* for quite some time.

'In 1931 (I think the year is correct), Romsey Borough Council elections were fought on a 'buckets or no buckets' campaign.

60

Many houses in Romsey have former privies in their back gardens.

As it made its daily run through the town, the chariot bore the legend 'Vote for buckets and keep our jobs'. The buckets lost and Romsey had a sewage farm. I believe the chariot men were re-sited there and found the end product delivered automatically with no effort on their part, so I suppose nobody really lost.'

Don Smith also experienced the Romsey chariot. He lived in Love Lane from the early 1920s. 'Our privy was a double, shared with a neighbour and some thirty yards up the garden path. Always in pristine condition, with neatly cut squares of newspaper suspended by a piece of string from a hook, it represented a haven of peace.

'On the morning that buckets were due to be emptied into the tanker, windows and doors were firmly closed until well after the vehicle had passed, and buckets cleaned and replaced.

'The men performing this operation were always regarded with sympathy and kindness in recognition of a job well done.

61

This ancient Botley farmhouse has undergone many alterations. I am assured that the extension on the left, not too far from the kitchen door, was once the privy.

Way down the garden path, two slate-roofed 'back to back' bucket privies at Catisfield. One door intact, the other on the ground, each with V notches for ventilation.

This may have been taken to extreme by a lady living in the centre of a terrace in Middlebridge Street. The story goes that she offered him passage through her kitchen and living room to the main street, to save himself a long walk round the back to the end of the terrace when carrying a full bucket.

'Furthermore, it was said, she sometimes offered him a cup of tea, bade him set his bucket down for a moment and suggested he have a little rest. It would not surprise me. We were a generous and tolerant lot.'

My old pal Dennis told me that if visitors filled the bucket before the Hurstbourne Priors violet cart was due to call, 'Dad took a sort of bowl with a handle and baled out the excess water onto the garden. The smell from our privy was never too special but in the summer and on emptying nights it was awful. I cringed with embarrassment when I brought a girlfriend home for the first time in 1957. She came from a modern home with a flush loo. I could see she was not terribly impressed with our old bucket, but she did marry me.'

Daphne Kingsland rented a Hampshire cottage, complete with outdoor privy, in 1963. She dreaded the 'bucket men' calling. 'It was so embarrassing - there was a bus stop immediately outside our gate, usually with several people waiting there.'

Even on vacation there was no escaping the honeycart. By coincidence, two ladies independently told me about their holidays at Naish Farm, Highcliffe, during the 1950s. Mrs Vickers of Eastleigh remembers its hundreds of wooden bungalows, many of them converted railway carriages. Their back-garden privies were wooden sheds, about the size of a telephone box, containing a bucket with a seat and a lid.

'On the front of each bungalow hung a wooden triangle, painted green on one side and red on the other. You turned the

This 100-year-old cottage at Horton Heath wasn't on mains sewerage. Visiting it after the elderly lady resident had left, all I found in the whitewashed privy by the back door was a piece of carpet, a toilet roll and a plastic bucket without a seat. Very strange.

triangle to show red when your bucket needed emptying. The bucket man spotted this as he toured the site with his horse and cart about twice a week. He would go in with a bucket in each hand, empty your bucket into these and so into his cart. Some say it was an open cart, but I don't think anyone got close enough to be sure. You turned the triangle back to green when he had gone.

'I remember the children would run indoors, shouting "The bucket man's coming!" and then watch him from behind the curtains.'

Elsie Brown of Hythe had an adventure that was more common than she might suppose while on holiday in one of those old railway carriages. 'One morning I had just got settled on the seat when the bucket disappeared from under me. I was so embarrassed that I just sat there until they had emptied the bucket and replaced it. I stayed in the shed until I was sure the area was cleared. When I went back inside and awoke my husband he could not stop laughing and still does when he thinks of it.'

Iris Gover grew up at Mill Farm in Mousehole Lane, Shirley, before the Second World War. Their pit privy had no door and stood in a long, open-fronted shed, with the chickens on one side and wood and coal on the other. After each performance, the soiled newspaper was burned (there was always an enamel candlestick with a box of matches), then waste soapy water was swished around the open-bottomed, porcelain bowl with a long-handled, stiff brush.

'There were three in our family, so the pit needed emptying only twice a year. Mr Scammel from Swaythling would be sent for, using one of his pre-printed postcards that said his services were "urgently needed", and he came with his horse and cart on clear, moonlit nights. We called him The Moonlight Man.

'He used a long handle with a bucket-type bowl on the end. He spread the contents on the fields, then in daylight we rolled it in with a heavy horse-roller. There was no paper to litter the fields, remember, because we had burnt it.'

Hursley was a do-it-yourself village, according to an elderly inhabitant I encountered there. About forty to forty-five years ago, workers from the Hursley Estate would dig a huge trench in a chalk pit in Port Lane - 'right where the bungalows are now!' he added mischievously. Householders dutifully carried their brimming buckets through the village streets and up the steep lane (which must have provided a delightful rustic spectacle) and when the trench eventually reached capacity another was prepared.

'There was a chap once, came home drunk as a lord. His missus was furious because she'd been waiting for him to empty the bucket. So off he went towards the chalk pit, ever so slow, trying his damnedest not to spill any, but he was that drunk he fell over in Port Lane. They found him on his knees, scraping up every last bit with his bare hands to put back in the bucket.'

It's not Hampshire, but I must mention Pauline Thompson's recollection of the terrifying 'night service' on Mauritius. Picture this high-sided, open lorry, festooned inside and out with dozens of filled privy buckets on hooks, all rattling and swaying and splashing anyone foolhardy enough to stand too close. It careered through the night, seemingly out of control, for fifteen miles downhill to Port Louis, there to unload whatever remained in the buckets. Our honeycarts sound tame by comparison.

[7]

MEET THE PROFESSIONALS

Wherever I went in Hampshire, people recalled their privy or cesspit being emptied by 'the cart from Botley'. They meant Hampshire Cleansing Service, a vigorous little business founded by Edgar 'Bunny' Hart with an 800-gallon tanker lorry bought second-hand for five pounds. He had six tankers by 1939, barely enough to tackle the thousands of buckets and pits filled by the multitude of military personnel who began pouring into Hampshire.

Built to collect 800 gallons of sewage, this Dennis tanker from about 1938 has a grab-rail behind the cab, a hatch for emptying buckets, and is painted a tasteful chocolate brown. Botley 139 was the telephone number.

Small, elliptically shaped tankers with convenient rear hatch and step-up were designed at Botley for speedy bucket emptying at wartime camps. Here, a post-war 400-gallon Thames tanker collects buckets at Tripps End caravan site in Hedge End.

With up to 200 buckets in each camp, Hart's vital but hitherto unsung contribution to the war effort eventually required a fleet of fifteen specially-built bucket-emptying vehicles and twenty more for the cesspits, all working seven days a week to meet the relentless demand. Never was so much muck shifted from so many by so few.

After the war 'the cart from Botley' was a familiar and welcome sight as Bunny Hart's business grew and diversified to become Cleansing Service Group, probably the biggest privately owned waste disposal company in the British Isles.

Herbert 'Slim' Pitman from Hedge End joined the firm at the age of 14, was 65 when he retired in 1994, stands six feet four inches in his bare feet and so was its longest serving employee in more senses than one. Slim emptied thousands of buckets, earth closets and cesspits during those fifty-one years, sometimes driving his tanker as far as Cheddar or Burnham-on-Sea and back to Botley in a day. He told me how the slopping buckets had to be heaved up onto a step at the back of the tanker and poured into its hatch, before the introduction of suction hoses made the task easier.

One of his most memorable jobs began with an urgent but seemingly routine request from Social Services to empty the bucket of an elderly lady who lived alone in Kings Worthy. She was nowhere to be seen when Slim arrived in the pouring rain but, oddly, the brimming receptacle sat waiting on her doorstep.

'I carried the bucket to the tanker, sucked everything out and cleaned it for her,' Slim told me. 'When I took it back there was another full bucket, so I did the same with that. Then blow me if she hadn't refilled the first one by the time I went to her door again.'

When a fourth bucket appeared, he banged on the door. An overpowering stink wafted from within as the old lady opened the door just a crack.

'Have you got much more?' Slim asked in exasperation. Her reply floored him nearly as much as the smell. 'Yes - half a bath full!'

Rejecting his offer to go inside and suck it dry with his long hose, she asked him to wait, then closed the door. 'When I looked through the window, she was dragging a long, tin bath into the kitchen with it all swilling about inside. I had to run the pipe up to the kitchen door and suck it out of the bath from there.'

As he stood in the April rain, Slim's astonishment was complete when the old lady apologised, 'I'm sorry about this. I haven't been able to get out all winter . . .'

Straight from the privy to the pasture, another load of ripe sewage gushes onto a farmer's field. Now forbidden, such disposal methods were commonplace well into the 1960s, raising bumper crops while lending a distinctive aroma to the countryside.

Problems could arise when emptying pits, says Slim. If there was no rear access, it meant trailing the tanker's suction pipe right through the house or shop - their customers just had to step round it. And many a crusty old pit needed dilution with buckets of water before its solidified contents were sloppy enough to pass through the pipe.

Finding somewhere to empty a full tanker was the driver's responsibility. 'The boss didn't want to know. It was down to you,' Slim explained. Fortunately, most farmers were only too pleased to have a load of untreated human manure spread over their fields. Dumping restrictions were lax in the old days. 'It was just a question of asking where they wanted it. My mate would open a valve at the back of the tanker then stand well clear. The stuff shot out to the side, perhaps three or four yards, while I drove around the field until the tank was empty.

'The farmers didn't pay us. We were doing each other a favour - we had to get rid of it somewhere and they wanted it. We might get a bit of produce, eggs and so on, perhaps a goose or a turkey at Christmas.'

At Hursley House near Winchester, the sewage had to be pumped from huge underground chambers covered with three lids. Slim and his mate, Tom Taylor, sweated for some time to remove the first, obstinate lid, after which Tom enjoyed a well-earned cigarette. Then he casually tossed his glowing fag-end into the open chamber. Now, decomposing sewage gives off methane gas, and great amounts of sewage produce great amounts of gas . . .

Slim says he will never forget that explosion, nor the sight of the other two lids, blown from their mountings, soaring high towards the sky.

Neither has he forgiven the owner of a restaurant at Ampfield, who telephoned a frantic plea for help in retrieving his false teeth, flushed down the loo and presumably trapped in their septic tank. Slim raced to the scene, ran out his trusty suction pipes, carefully drew off the tank's watery contents and peered inside. No teeth. So he clambered down into the darkness to remove the remaining thick sludge by hand, examining each savoury shovelful by the light of his torch. No teeth. They must have been sucked up into the tanker.

Determined not to be beaten, Slim emerged into the fresh air to tell the gummy restaurateur his plan. He would drive to an emptying field and somehow fit a sieve over his tanker's outlet pipe to trap those elusive gnashers.

As he set off, the man's wife came rushing out. 'You needn't bother,' she shouted up to the cab. 'He's found them. They were in his back pocket all along!'

Joe Goodyear of St Mary Bourne didn't enjoy such luxuries as a tanker lorry and suction pipes. For some 35 years he emptied privy buckets using nothing more than a huge iron tumbler, like an enormous barrel slung between two wheels, drawn through the country lanes by a horse and later by a tractor. He reckons it weighed about two tons when fully laden with ordure. Turning a small wheel operated a chain to slowly tip it up for emptying.

Joe learned his trade by working with his father, George, who for many years was contracted by Kingsclere and Whitchurch District Council to 'remove night soil' in St Mary Bourne, Stoke and Hurstbourne Priors. 'In the end, father asked if I thought I could manage by myself and I said yes,' he told me.

From the late 1930s the big tumbler was drawn by George's horse, a powerful beast that once pulled guns for the army and still bore the military broad arrow and regimental number on his rump. When Joe came out of the army himself, in 1947, they got a tractor instead.

But I'll let Joe tell his own story. 'We were supposed to be the night cart. The council said we shouldn't start before ten at night but people didn't want to wait up and unlock their sheds for us. Half the time the karzies were in their coal houses and they kept them locked. There were even some indoors buckets, like the one at the post office. It was up the stairs and we had to carry everything downstairs.

'So father told the council and they said to ask people when they wanted us to call. Well, half of them said, "The earlier you comes the bloody better, George", so that's what we done. We used to go out about half past seven and we're back home half past nine or quarter to ten.

73

A typical bucket privy on Joe Goodyear's round at Hurstbourne Priors. Note the ventilation space above the door, and the adjoining store for coal and wood.

'We'd take two empty pails up to the karzies and pour the muck into them to save going up and down the gardens, otherwise you'd have been at it all night, but some of their buckets held so much we still had to make two trips. If it was a bit watery, father used to say, "Stand it on the garden, boy, and drain it off - just take the solids."

'Funny thing, the buckets never froze up, even in the coldest weather. Just round the edges, perhaps, but that's all.

'At the start there was no lid on the cart so it used to slop out a bit. While I was away in the army a couple of blokes helped father and instead of sitting on the shafts of the cart they sat on a board across the top of the tumbler. One night one of them slipped off and went straight in. After that they had a lid, hinged in the middle so half would open to pour the buckets in.

'Of course it used to smell. People closed their windows when they heard us coming but it wasn't as bad as some made out. There was a nice couple in the village, a retired RAF officer, and they would walk past quite happily and wish us a good evening but others would go over the other side of the road and make a show of holding their noses and screwing up their faces.

'We emptied the tumbler in the farmers' fields, building it up until it was about eight feet deep. Ashes, straw or other stuff was mixed in, then it was left to settle. You could see it going down gradually, week by week, as the water eased out.

'Eventually the farmer would spread it over his land and plough it in. By then you wouldn't have known what it was. There was no smell and it didn't show no paper nor nothing, but tomatoes used to sprout up all over the fields.

Another Hurstbourne Priors privy, almost hidden by shrubs, flowers and climbing roses.

'My two nephews aged about eight and ten visited us from Birmingham once and we took them up to the fields where we were harvesting. They'd never been in the country before. They played about for a while but then they dashed across and jumped into what they thought was just a big pile of straw. We shouted but it was too late. They sank right down into all that muck.

'God, it was evil! We took them home and my missus took one look and said, "Right, you can strip off outside the door!"'

'One old gentleman who never had his bucket emptied won all the prizes at the flower show. His vegetables were great, too. Plenty of other people used to keep it for the garden. The old boys used to dig it in, every Friday night. In those days we had good, wholesome food, everything was really worth having, but not now the crops are all treated with chemicals.'

Joe was quiet for a while. Then he sighed wistfully. 'Ah, they were good old days. But after they were put on the mains, folk said we don't need the karzi now, we'll take it down and use that wood for something else, perhaps build some chicken houses. I suppose they chucked the buckets out for scrap.'

[8]

SEATS OF LEARNING

Too many of Hampshire's old privy buildings have been torn down without a thought for their place in history. I discovered a precious exception in Itchen Stoke, behind the former schoolhouse where Peter Wixon has lived since the age of five. His father was granted the tenancy of the house during the 1930s as neither of the village's two teachers wanted to live there, so young Peter's daily trip to school meant simply popping next door!

Until their indoors loo was installed in about 1947, the Wixon

The former Itchen Stoke school privies, with separate girls' and boys' entrances. Teachers and the family who rented the schoolhouse shared the single-bucket end privy (with ventilation notches above the door).

'Behind the bogs' at Itchen Stoke school. Its bucket flaps have been bricked-up, the draughty louvre windows glazed, but the pump (in the centre) has been spared. It fed a roof tank for two hand basins.

family had to share the teachers' bucket at the end of the privies in the school playground. There were also three boys' cubicles and three for the girls. These seven buckets guaranteed Peter's father a regular supply of goodness as he willingly undertook to bury their valuable contents in his vegetable garden alongside the playground.

A hand pump behind the privies filled a roof tank to feed two basins, one each for the girls and boys to wash their hands in cold water.

Everyone who told me about their school privies recalled them with a mixture of fascination and revulsion. They were usually outside in the playground, often open to the elements, draughty, smelly, wet and unwelcoming. Here was none of the wistful nostalgia often associated with the privy back home. Nobody had a kind word for the old school bogs.

When Denise Graham of Alton started school at Micheldever County Primary in 1953, she found the facilities unchanged since her mother had been a pupil there during the early 1930s.

'We had three privies, one for the girls, one for the boys and one for the two teachers. There was no running water, just a pump, and we had to wash our hands in the classroom with an enamel jug and basin. We used to be given the allotted two pieces of scratchy toilet paper by the teacher when we needed to go.

'The privies were under a yew tree in the playground, with doors that let in all the rain, wind and snow, but no light, so when you shut the door you were in the dark.

'They used to pong somewhat in the summer. The highlight of our week was when the "stink bomb lorry" arrived from Botley to empty away the unmentionables. We used to hope it was play-time, when we could all watch.

'The privies were replaced with flush loos in about 1955-56 but still in the same building and still with no lights. It is there to this day.'

Miss Halfacre, who during the war attended the Crescent Primary in Eastleigh, also discovered that 'there was no paper in the toilet blocks. Any child who needed some had to ask the teacher, who would take a roll of Bronco-Izal type paper from a cupboard in the classroom.'

'It seems incredible that we have had sanitation in our village only in the last fifty years,' says Muriel O'Grady from Ash, near Aldershot. 'This was a very rural area and even in the school we had to go outside the main building to a brick built block at the edge of the playground. It housed the toilets, those dreadful buckets enclosed in wooden frame seats with drop-down fronts which enabled the buckets to be removed for emptying. I think

Pupils at Newtown Soberton Infant School probably don't realise that their pretty 'Wendy House' was originally a privy, possibly reserved for the village teacher who lived in the nearby schoolhouse.

we had progressed at school from newspaper squares to a block of fawn coloured, ridged paper. It was more like cardboard.'

At least some schools tried to reduce the smells caused by uncovered buckets. Peat, being absorbent, plentiful and cheap, was often thrown onto the contents. Percy Lucas of Woolston, Southampton, even enjoyed the novelty of automatic peat closets at North Stoneham School, which is now the Concorde Club. 'The girls' and boys' toilets were separated by a long building where firewood and peat were stored. Each toilet cubicle contained a bucket and a huge container filled with peat.

'The seats were made of wood, scrubbed so regularly they were almost white. It was like sitting on a large wooden box. When one sat on the seat it moved downwards and upon rising it shot back up again, releasing the necessary amount of peat into the bucket. We used newspaper, cut into squares, threaded on string and hung up in the toilet.

'Mr Fudge used to dispose of the contents, I imagine once a week, at the bottom of the school playground. There was an area of ground fenced off, with a wicket gate, where huge pits were dug to empty the buckets.

'The boys' urinal was also in the yard. There was no cover over it, so one used it regardless of the elements. All the urine ran down a sloping trough into the river.'

Beryl Matthews of Netley Abbey, Southampton, and her sister Louisa remember the peat buckets at Locks Heath Council School, 'a whole row of smelly privies where the wind blew up, and down. It was the only place to play if it was wet in the dinner hour, because the classrooms were kept locked.

'The privies were always painted grey and had slatted doors which the children used to climb on, sitting right up on top some-times because the doors didn't reach the ceiling. It is no wonder that they were often hanging off. There were small windows in these buildings and some of the more adventurous boys used to climb through them at play times and hope they were not caught.

'The buckets were filled up to about half way with peat. If we dropped something down the hole, there it stayed. There was no retrieving it, the hole was too deep. They were emptied every night, way down in a field behind the school.'

The lavatories at Hurstbourne Priors village school were in a building made of flint stones, recalls my friend Dennis, who was there between 1945 and 1951. 'The boys' urinal was a trough filled with peat, but for "bigger jobs" there were holes cut in a long wooden seat and partitioned off. There were no buckets under those seats. From time to time a man from the village would arrive with his wheelbarrow and go through a door on the side of the building. It led to beneath both the girls' and boys' toilets. He would work away down there, shovelling everything into his wheelbarrow, add the peat from the urinal and dump it all on a heap on some waste land near the school. Later on, a tractor and trailer would collect the whole stinking mess and take it to who knows where.'

The privies could be a truly frightening place for a child, as this lady experienced when she began school in 1937 at St George Street Infants in Portsmouth.

'The girls' toilets consisted of about five or six partitioned cubicles in an outside, brick built block. The doors would rarely stay closed, so anyone could come along while one was using the loo and say, "Look at this one!" to a crowd of other girls. One long bench ran through all the cubicles and in each of them was a big round hole that seemed large enough for any small child to fall through. All the wooden seating areas were well soiled with urine and not at all inviting to climb up and sit upon.

'Beneath the seats was a large "river" which varied in colour but was usually quite thick and brown with goodness knows what. On one of the days when I really had to use the toilet, I was terrified by a loud rushing sound of running water beneath me which I quite thought would be life-threatening. Presumably some clean water was flushed through the whole area from time to time but it could not have been very often, judging by the state of the toilets.

'I only used them a few times. Often I would go in but only pretend to have used them. This sometimes resulted in an unfortunate accident before home time, so I was not very popular in those days, either with school or my parents.

'To this day, I still sometimes have frightening dreams about old lavatories.'

Equally dreadful memories came from Joyce Stevens, who

described the conditions at Headley, the Holme, Church of England School in the 1920s. 'Yes, the lavatories were horrendous but that was common to all the schools in the district because we had no public sewerage system. There were two playgrounds, one for the boys, the other for girls, so the lavatories were also separate. I dreaded using them. They had individual cubicles with wooden seats but my memory is that the seats were usually wet, the floor swimming in urine from the over-flowing buckets, and excrement not always in the right place because small children hadn't got there in time. The smell was awful.

'My oldest friend lived a mile from the school and went home to dinner at midday. Her mother used to make her children spend a penny the very last thing before walking to school and urged them to avoid using the school conveniences unless desperate.

'One very vivid memory is of poor, sobbing children standing in pools of warm urine in the classroom because they hadn't asked to "be excused" in time. I was obsessed and terrified that it might happen to me - thank God it never did. The strange thing is that we were all remarkably healthy, except for occasional epidemics of measles or influenza.

'I am told that conditions were the same at Bordon Council School in the mid 1950s. They had Bronco toilet paper then, but squares of newspaper were used in my day. What progress!'

As if all this wasn't enough to endure, little girls often had to be extra wary when settling upon the seat. They made tempting targets. Tales abound of the pranks played by naughty boys, usually involving the unexpected application of stinging nettles to defenceless bums.

When Ernest Davey's father retired from the Royal Marines in the mid 1930s they moved to Clanfield, where, he says, 'I was sentenced to attend the village school. The loos were an open pit

Isolated rural churches had to take care of their congregations' earthly needs, too. These privies behind the 19th-century Soberton Methodist Church had at least been upgraded to an Elsan closet!

with timber cubicles over. The boys' and girls' sheds were quite close together and I recall fearsome stories of the undesirables being lowered into the pit, armed with stinging nettles, and sneaking across to beneath the girls' cubicles to cause mayhem. I never took part but listened with great awe to the tales told by the alleged culprits.'

Rosa Johnson of Titchfield tells me of a school where the boys made good use of an abundant supply of nettles growing by the fence, stuffing them between the wooden panels of the girls' privies at a height carefully estimated to be Seated Bottom Level.

Finally, to demonstrate that even the staff were not immune from attack, Barrie Wateridge of Cadnam tells this lovely story about his Uncle Fred. He used to attend Copythorne School, where the outside lavatories were earth buckets with flaps along the back of the building for access to empty them.

'One morning, it seems, Fred was chastised by his lady teacher. Bent on revenge, in the dinner hour he purloined a feather
duster from somewhere in the school and removed the flap from
the back of the ladies' cubicle. Then he waited quietly for the
teacher to enter, whereupon he inserted the feather duster and
a hilarious group of children watched her bolt from the door,
screaming, unable to run as her drawers were round her ankles.

'Fred had two hidings, one at school and another when he
arrived home with a letter from the headmaster. Even so, he
said, he was a hero for weeks.'

[9]

WARTIME WOES

Many of the children who were evacuated to Hampshire's inland villages during the Second World War faced a culture shock. Raised in urban houses with unlimited water on tap and indoor lavatories that flushed clean with a pull of the chain, the youngsters were thrust rudely into a strange world of country smells, pumps and wells.

And privies.

'It was my first and only encounter with an outside privy. I will never forget it,' wrote one lady. As a ten-year-old, she was evacuated from Southampton to Timsbury with her younger brother. 'We were sent to live with a very nice couple in a terraced cottage. By the time we arrived I was bursting to use the toilet. The lady said, "It's out the back, usual place", but all I found was a little wooden shed. When I went back indoors and told her she laughed and explained that this dirty shed was actually their only toilet. I was horrified. I couldn't believe such things existed.

'Being small, we had to seat ourselves carefully over the big hole and hang on tightly to avoid falling through. No bucket, everything just plopped down into a big pit and piled up. I hated it.

'On the wall above the seat was a framed religious text that read NEARER MY GOD TO THEE.'

Evacuated to Stockbridge with her two-year-old son, Mrs Pudney of Southampton found the usual chamber pot under their bed. 'First thing in the morning I would empty it into the privy bucket. After a few days my landlady ticked me off for filling the bucket, which was emptied weekly. "You should empty

A charming piece of England's heritage, neatly tucked away in a garden at Kingsclere.

All self-respecting households had chamber pots under the beds to avoid night-time treks down the garden path. Ronald Hansford's collection of sanitary memorabilia also includes a men's combination bed pan (right) and a slipper bed pan (top).

the potty over the gooseberries" she said.'

Fortunately, not everyone had a bad time. Here's what David Philpot from South Wonston told me: 'My brother John and I were evacuated from Southsea to Dean Farm Cottages in South Warnborough in 1940. We were billeted with Jack and Emily Rampton.

'They were one of a terrace of three cottages and the only mains service was a cold water tap in the kitchen/living room. Our privy was a sectioned-off part of the woodshed which ran behind the cottages. Jack emptied the bucket in the garden, in a trench which the following year he would use to grow his runner beans.

'He rode everywhere on his bicycle, wearing a pork pie hat, a

Instructions on the 19th-century slipper bed pan read: 'This Slipper should be passed under the Patient in front between the legs. If a flannel cap is made for the blade, fastened by strings under the handle, considerable comfort will be afforded'.

broadcloth poacher's jacket and breeches with leather boots and gaiters. Normally his boots and gaiters were black but for Sundays and special occasions he had a best brown set which were so highly polished you could see your face in them.

'He worked as a jobbing gardener during the day but in the evenings and at weekends he was the village hairdresser for men and boys, with his "shop" in the woodshed. That is when our visits to the loo next door were very interesting, as we could overhear the conversations between him and his customers while trying to be as quiet as possible, not always successfully because the privy door squeaked as it was opened.'

Another evacuee, John Ramsier of Gosport, has this wonderful wartime memory. 'The house we were sent to was near Winchester, with a privy at the bottom of a long garden where they kept all sorts of livestock, as people were encouraged to do in the war. We had never seen one before, so it never occurred to us that everything that went into the bucket had to be emptied by hand. After a few days the man took Peter (my brother) and me to one side and said we had to stop filling the bucket so quickly - if we only wanted a pee, we should do it behind a bush in the garden.

'All went well until the day I examined the bucket after use and saw it was getting full. Worried in case we got the blame, we resolved to bury it in the garden, as we had seen the man do, while the couple were out.

'The bucket is almost as big as us and damned heavy. We each take a side of the handle and stagger away up the path with the evil brew slopping between us. As we pass the pigsty, a pig suddenly pokes its head over the wall with a grunt, Peter jumps back startled and I fall over with the whole bucketload on top of me.

'I can still smell it now. I was covered in it. I had to get cleaned up before they got home, so I went and jumped in the river, clothes and all. Then I stripped naked and washed all the muck out of my clothes. Peter had the worse job, using bits of wood and paper to scrape the unmentionable off the path back into the bucket.

'We dared not tell our hosts what had really happened, so we pretended I had fallen in the river. They were most concerned. They even gave us sixpence as a reward for emptying the bucket.'

The privations of those youngsters as they discovered the dubious delights of rural sanitation were naught compared with the sufferings back home. As Hitler's bombers nightly attacked Hampshire, even the bravest heart could be challenged by the humble act of visiting the privy, once a haven of peace and contemplation.

For Iris Gover, using the outside loo of the Old Thatch in

Shirley, Southampton (where, she remembers wistfully, they did a good glass of cowslip wine), was an adventure in itself during the blackout.

'I'm sure it was a bucket out there. You had to go down a passage, feeling your way along the outside wall in the pitch dark. In a hurry one night, I rushed in and there was a woman already on the seat in the blackness. She began screaming but it was too late. I peed on her. I dashed back inside the pub, which was lit up, and soon this loud voice was saying angrily, "Where is she? I'll kill the bugger!" I was wet myself, of course, but I kept very quiet and got away with it.'

Betty Wells had an even more harrowing experience, counting herself lucky to be living still in Hedge End, where at the age of eleven or twelve she experienced her most traumatic visit to the privy.

'It had to be 1940 or 41. The air-raid sirens had gone. It was after dark and us kids were all taking cover under the big kitchen table (this was before the Anderson or Morrison shelters). We had a family from Woolston who came to sleep at our house to get a little further away from Southampton docks, which were a target for Jerry. The men were all outside on fire watch, Jerry planes with their horrible throbbing engines were overhead, and I had to go to the lav. My stomach used to churn so much I didn't know if I wanted to spend a penny, be sick or what, but the only place for any of it was the lav.

'We didn't have to go down the garden path, it was attached to the house, but nevertheless it was outside, a big bucket and wooden seat type. My mum took me out there to make sure I didn't show any light for Jerry to see. As I lifted the latch to go in, I heard my brother shout, "It's a bloody parachute!" and immediately somebody else said, "There's another one!" By now I was scared stiff, I thought we were being invaded.

'Well, I managed to spend my penny and was about to

retrieve my drawers when there was an almighty explosion and the world caved in on me. It seemed as though it was the whole house coming down but actually it was only the ceiling. I really thought my number was up. I did look a sorry sight, covered in slats of wood, bits of the wall and plaster, and although it was very frightening at the time all the family had a good laugh afterwards at my being "plastered".

'The damage to our house and privy wasn't too bad but a big house on the top of Sunday's Hill was demolished and a young lad was killed. It wasn't Germans on those parachutes. It was land mines.'

Pauline Thompson's equally alarming tale of the perils of the privy during those dreadful days came with the earnest assurance, 'This is a true story - it really happened.' She was stationed in a small village in 1941/42, billeted in a cottage which enjoyed a smart privy with a wide, scrubbed wooden seat. Well, it did until the fickle finger of fate intervened.

'One evening, my landlady of advanced years and large in size took a needy walk down the garden path to the privy, set amidst lovely flowers with a background of a narrow green valley with trees either side, fading into the beautiful sunset. Alas, this scene of bliss was soon to be shattered by German bombers flying overhead. Distant explosions could be heard, then the planes flew back from their target, unloading their unwanted bombs.

'Concern was being felt for the poor woman within the privy, when all at once a bomb dropped nearby. The blast blew the privy backwards, leaving my bewildered and shocked landlady still sitting with such grace and dignity upon the undamaged privy seat, the sky her ceiling and the privy structure laying upside down some few yards away.

'My landlord rushed to her aid. Being crippled with back problems he found lifting her off the seat hard work. She gazed up at the sky in wonderment: a few moments ago she was sitting safely in her own mini world in peace and quiet, and then her world had opened up in a rush.

'Poor soul died three weeks later, of other natural causes, not the bomb blast.'

Further confirmation that the wartime privy afforded no sanctuary comes in this cautionary tale, related to me by a gentleman in Andover. 'My Uncle Jim never tired of telling me of the time he was on leave from the army with my dad and their mate. They went out for a few pints, all in their uniforms, and while they were in the pub the snow fell deep upon the ground.

'Just before closing time father had to use the privy, a little sentry-box affair in the pub garden with a big bucket and an emptying flap at the back. He was still in residence when the others came out of the pub, rather the worse for wear. After a while they got fed up waiting in the cold and began shouting for my dad to hurry up. Finally their mate said, "This'll shift the bugger", lifted the flap and threw in a big thunderflash (a powerful firework used by the army on training exercises).

'The explosion ripped the flap from its hinges. The front door flew open and out shot father in a cloud of smoke, tripped over his braces and rolled about in the snow, cursing and swearing, holding his ringing head with one hand while trying to pull up his trousers with the other. Uncle Jim and the other bloke were helpless with laughter, shouting things like, "Blimey, Harry, that was a loud one! What you been drinking?"

'Uncle Jim always used to end this story by saying, "It was a daft thing to do, really. If that big iron bucket hadn't saved your dad's tackle from being blown clean off, you wouldn't be sitting here listening to this tale." '

[1 0]

HAMPSHIRE HOGS ON HAMPSHIRE BOGS

There used to be an 'adult and child' two-holer at West Wellow village hall. It had served nobly for as long as anyone could remember, so when the hall was demolished in the 1970s some sentimental person had the notion of saving its venerable seat for posterity. Solemnly auctioned to raise funds for the Scouts, it now enjoys honourable retirement in a private museum at Romsey.

Underlying this tale is a moral. Privies were not to be sniffed at in disgust: to get the best out of them, you really needed a sense of the ridiculous.

That garden dunnekin was all you had to go on, so you might just as well try to see its funny side - like Marian Hunt's husband, whose aunt displayed this earnest request within her privy at Burley in the New Forest:

> After using the lavatory, please
> place one shovel of ashes and one
> handful of ferns inside bucket.

Or like Mrs Shepherd of Ropley, who knew a two-holer where a resourceful bantam which commandeered the smaller hole was left in peace to hatch a brood of chicks. Human and hen sat side by side, each engrossed in their own business.

Fortunately, people who enjoy being known as Hampshire Hogs are obviously robust enough to laugh at anything to do with their privy. Any doubts I might have had on that score disappeared under the deluge of delightful memories my fellow Hogs sent me when they heard that I was pursuing privies. I hope you, too, enjoy their stories. They remind us of a time

A bird-lover's privy at Upham. Below the nest-box is a square entrance hole with a landing platform. 'I converted the roof space into a little loft for a pigeon which had been hanging around the house for days,' the owner explained. 'The day after I completed the job, the pigeon took off and never came back.'

95

when everyday life, although sometimes hard and lacking the material comforts of today, seemed so much more pleasant, when families mattered and folk had time for their neighbours. It was only yesterday, yet a whole lifetime away.

Beryl Matthews of Netley Abbey grew up in Park Gate, where they had an 'awful' outside privy, with spiders, cobwebs, and candles in the winter. If it was occupied the children would nip through a hole in the hedge and use their grandparents' privy next door. 'Grandad didn't take kindly to this as it meant theirs filled up quicker,' she told me. 'I am sure their spiders were bigger, too.

'Mum used to keep us out of the way while Dad dug a hole to empty our bucket - frequently. We grew our own veg in the garden, good crops indeed, but it must have been a nightmare finding a fresh place to tip the waste, week after week.'

Even in her nineties, Dora Ackerman vividly remembers visiting an old lady in Ampfield at the age of seven and the pride she felt at being allowed to accompany her to the privy. 'There were three holes, a big one with smaller ones each side. The old lady, who was very stout, sat on the big one and I sat on one of the others, so we were both happy.'

When Dora had her own family and a bucket at Littleton, 'a rather posh lady' invited the children to tea, including three-year-old Bobby. Dora was mortified to be told next day, 'Your son spent most of his time in our toilet pulling the chain. When I suggested he stop it and play with the others, he said, "I like pulling this chain - we only got a bloody bucket." ' As Dora says, 'Bobby had heard his father call the bucket that when he had to empty it, so I couldn't scold him, could I?'

Mrs Legg lived in the first of eight houses in St Mary Bourne, which meant much to-ing and fro-ing by the night-cart men on

A bucket privy has stood in this Stockbridge garden for at least 88 years. This one, about 40 years old, was still in use in 1969. Its bucket was easily emptied - a little stream flows immediately behind.

Monday and Friday nights. 'As it all passed our house it was quite a smell. When my cousin came for summer holidays, the highlight of our evening was to look out of the bedroom window at the passing buckets of pong.

'My aunt had a better loo than ours, closed in, and as they were better off they used San-Izal more often. Ours was just a board across with a hole in it. Later my mum found a board to put down the front to shield the bucket. We used to save orange wrappers to ring the changes from newspaper.'

Joyce Stevens of Headley says their privy was in use well after World War II. 'This Wealden house was divided into three labourers' dwellings during the early 19th century, so once

Botley people have sensibly preserved many of their substantial old privy buildings. This one is in the garden of a house built in 1903.

there were three privies here. Each had a smooth wooden seat, a box for ashes to put in the bucket after each visit and squares of newspaper hanging by string from a nail.

'The oldest, used by the middle cottage, was at the far end of the garden, built of stone and brick, with a pitched clay-tiled roof, matching the house. It was forty-five yards from the house, so imagine the trek in bad weather on dark wintry nights, carrying a hurricane lamp. If the weather was kind, our neighbour made the journey carrying a candle-stick, shading the flame with her hand. This privy was right next to the pig sty.

'The north cottage also had a pig sty. Attached to it was a shed for wood and coal, and tucked away in a corner of this was a privy. It was only half-way down the long garden, and so when my great-aunt made her way down her path she might have been fetching coal or wood or a gardening tool for all anyone knew.

'Our privy was the newest and very close to our back door. It was shaped like a sentry-box, made of wood, with a concrete floor and two steps up to the door because of the slope of the garden. We called it The Telephone Box. I was grown up before it dawned upon me that we must have been unique in using the expression "going to the telephone" as our euphemism.'

'As a country girl, I certainly remember the old privies,' says Rosa Johnson of Titchfield. 'We still live out in the sticks and when the air is calm our septic tank smells just about the same as the privies did all those years ago.

'My grandparents lived in Laverstoke during the '30s and '40s. Their privy was only a one-holer but it was quite large, airy and clean. It always smelt of cereals, mainly the flaked maize that Grandad fed to his border collies.

'Rural folk didn't use toilet rolls in those days, so we had to make do with squares of glossy paper, something I never much liked. I think they were torn from *Picture Post* magazine. We children were not allowed to use the stiff bolt on the privy door - Granny used to say, "Just close the door and sing if you don't want to be disturbed."

'They lived too far off the map to have their bucket emptied by the council, so Grandad had to dispose of the contents (he called it "the soil") himself. I remember him carrying that big bucket down the garden to a trench which he gradually filled in through the winter months. Then he would level it up in March, ready to plant his runner beans in May.

'More fortunate folk had their buckets emptied at intervals by the council's "gully wagon" or "night cart" which toured the villages after dark. There was a junction at the bottom of a hill, called "Hobdiggin" by the locals, on the St Mary Bourne to

The pub privy at the Robin Hood in Durley inclines forward slightly. That's because a couple of drunken farm labourers backed their carthorse against it, according to one local yarn.

Whitchurch road, where the contents were tipped out in the fields and left to settle. We knew it as "Dirty Corner".

'Two cottages stood nearby and one day a district nurse, Nurse Gardner, having delivered a baby in one of them, asked to use their privy. When she realised how far it was she decided it might be quicker to jump into her car and drive to the nearest house with plumbing. It was a mile and a half away. I understand she just made it.

'The privy at my aunt's cottage in Vernham Dean was a fine three-holer near the end of her garden. Its biggest hole was just inside the door, so anyone sitting there could keep it shut with their foot. It was also rather cramped, which meant ample ladies like my aunt, wearing voluminous skirts, had difficulty lowering their bloomers inside with the door shut.

'Aunty overcame this problem by reversing carefully in through the doorway, dropping her drawers as she went. Once comfortably seated, she would close the door with her foot and proceed to business.

'A local tramp did some odd jobs at the cottage while I was staying with her once. She was making damson pies and said he could take a few in return. That night, snuggled in bed, I heard Aunty set off down the path on her customary last visit to the privy. Moments later a terrible commotion erupted in the garden, my aunt screaming blue murder and somebody shouting, and I jumped to the window in time to see her storming back to the cottage, hauling up her underwear as she came.

'When she had stopped trembling with indignation, she explained how she had backed in as usual, only to find herself sitting alongside the tramp, who was on the second hole, trousers round his ankles, not daring to move.

'He tried to say her pies had "upset his innards", but that only made her more cross. She reckoned he'd helped himself to too many raw damsons while she wasn't looking.

'Great-grandfather built it himself, at least 150 years ago,' said the lady in Upham who is preserving this family heirloom. 'It was a two-holer with a pit. One day, my sister and I were playing behind it with our angora rabbit when it slipped through the slats covering the pit and fell in. Dad had to fish it out and wash it. He wasn't too pleased.'

'I've often wondered who had the greater shock that night, Aunty at suddenly discovering she was not alone, or the old tramp, sitting there aghast as her great white backside reversed through the door in the moonlight.'

Tramps often borrowed privies for a crafty snooze. Old-time coppers, too, as police discipline records show. A typical case, before the Southampton Borough Watch Committee in 1852, finds PC Searle in trouble after his sergeant 'stated that he found Searle asleep in a privy at the Back of the Walls and that he looked for him previously for an hour before he found him. Searle in his defence said that he was in the privy but was suffering from a Bowel Complaint and fell asleep'.

Hampshire's village policemen usually had privies in their allotted houses. 'Most of the country beats had the same lack of amenities,' wrote policeman's daughter Muriel Garlike. 'I can recall in 1932 or 1933 when I was a young child my father was posted to Upton Grey. The police cottage is still there, next to the village hall. We had two wells, one for drinking, the other a tank of rain water. There was no electricity or gas and the loo was a shed up the garden with a boxed-in affair with a bucket, one for adults and a smaller one for a child. Father had the finest vegetables and fruit bushes, as the bucket was emptied into a pit and later used to fertilise the garden.'

Mrs Garlike herself married a policeman. 'We were posted to a new house at Oliver's Battery in Winchester in 1954, one of six with no mains sewerage. They shared a small sewage filtration plant at the bottom of our garden, which fascinated the children as there was a bar which used to go round and then tip over with a thud.'

The village bobby at Silchester had a fine view from his privy, recalls his friend and fellow policeman, Denis Padwick. 'Bill liked to do his little sitting jobs with the door open, at peace with the world, watching the cows in the field and listening to the lark. He was intrigued one day as to why some people walking along the lane at the far side of the field were looking intently in his direction. Then he realised that they had probably never before seen a policeman doing what comes naturally.'

Barbara St John's grandfather is said to have combined pleasure with business by exchanging gossip through the privy wall with his similarly-enthroned brother who lived next door. Their back-to-back privies in Hordle were actually on the boundary of their properties, so one of her aunts preferred to ride there on a bicycle she kept outside the back door.

'My father told me that when they built the outside toilet at our bungalow, the carpenter got one of my aunts to sit on a plank of wood,' says Barbara. 'Then he drew round her bottom for size before cutting out the hole.'

From Barrie Wateridge of Cadnam comes the tale of a day when 'Grandma and I were in the front garden of her cottage. A charabanc drew up and the driver asked to use the lavatory. She said yes, but was aghast when about thirty people piled off and queued for the outside privy. At least there was soon a smile on my face, as they pressed pennies into my hand. It was about half a crown in all, I think, indeed a fortune at the time.'

Ernest Davey discovered that his future in-laws' cottage near Clanfield 'had a deep well just outside the back door and close by a most friendly two-seater earth closet. This was used by the family as a normal event but I found it very difficult to adjust. About five-hundred yards down the lane, another family called the Trodds had the same type of services but their cottage was closer to the undergrowth and I recall old Mr Trodd moaning about having to clear adders out of the loo from time to time.'

A New Forest gentleman recalls his relatives' privy at Copythorne being so far from the house that on wet days people had to don macs and wellies for the trip. 'My late uncle would often read his newspaper in this loo if no one needed to use it for a while,' he added.

'Other relatives had a farm at Winsor, where the privy overlooked an open view of meadows, hedgerows and a stile. Many people would leave its door open to enjoy the view and the fresh air.'

Here's a hair-raising anecdote from Jim Knight of Alton. 'The outside dunny at my guardian's house was a flimsy wooden structure tacked on to the end of a brick outhouse, right alongside the main Alton to Bordon road at Kingsley. Doing one's duty could be a bit of an adventure, as large vehicles passed at a fair speed, making the whole structure rock alarmingly. One didn't linger too long in there.

'The edifice was, to say the least, well ventilated, with gaps at bottom and top of the door, and numerous holes where knots had fallen out of the shiplap boarding. This was handy if anyone one knew passed by, because one could hail a cheerful greeting between grunts.

'This dunny came to a spectacular end when a reckless motorist lost control and slammed right into it, demolishing the whole structure. The mind boggles at what might have transpired had the thing been in use at the time but luckily they had an inside loo by then.'

Another risky affair was using the sawmill privies at British Rail's Eastleigh Carriage Works, according to Ron Cordall of Romsey.

He was apprenticed there in the mid '40s and remembers its long row of ten or twelve partitioned privy holes over a common trough which, when full, emptied away automatically at one end. Fresh water flowed in from the other end after about half a minute, time enough for mischievous apprentices to ignite a large ball of newspaper and float it downstream on the incoming tide beneath unsuspecting backsides. 'Can you imagine the noise and the panic?' says Ron. 'What fun for the youngsters, though!'

The pleasure of dressing up in your finery for an evening out was marred when the only loo was a bucket, outside in the cold rain - but that's how it used to be, as Mr Chase reminds us. 'Tytherly village hall was not connected until about 1970. The cricket club always held its dinner dances there. I supplied cable and light so the ladies could find their way to the little hut some twenty yards away, although they had to manage without a light within. The men used the wood on the other side of the village hall.'

Mr Chase also remembers an old soldier who had to make do with an outdoor closet as late as 1970. 'I often spoke to him while he cleaned his bucket - polished it, in fact - before hanging it upside down on a post, ready for use. I assumed this was the result of his army training.'

Mr Honeybun of Brockenhurst says that only when absolutely necessary was the 'large hole' beneath his grandparents' privy at Houghton emptied, by horse and cart. But what surprised him was that between this cesspit and their house stood the well which supplied their drinking water, its level only about eight feet down. 'The mind boggles,' he says, 'yet that water was lovely, clear and fresh tasting.'

'I had the misfortune to spend my first week of married life in a house with a privy,' recalls Jill McPhail. 'That was in 1966, in a cottage owned by Strong's Brewery in the Horsefair at Romsey. My first encounter with it was at night. It was at the bottom of the garden so I was given a torch, but once inside I had a problem: what to do with the torch. Should it be placed on the floor or in my teeth? No problem for men, but women have more awkward clothing to deal with and going to the loo requires two hands at some stages. I think I compromised by sticking it under my armpit.'

Progress may have put paid to the privy at the bottom of the garden but the modern loo has brought its own challenges.

Getting a flush toilet on their farm at Longdown after thirty years of buckets and pits meant Iris Gover had to cope with water metering. 'My husband, a down-to-earth farmer, could not bear to think that if anyone only went to wee they flushed away three gallons of water he had to pay for. So when visitors wanted to use the loo, he'd ask, "Big jobs or small? If it's only small, pee in the stable or cowshed drain."

'I felt awful when he said this, but that water bill could mount up with a lot of summer visitors.'

When a new door was fitted to this beauty near Whiteley, fresh heart-holes were vital - because bats had taken up residence. It still had its two-holer seat in 1990, one large and one small hole, with two buckets. 'The council asked if I wanted it knocked down. I wouldn't let them,' says the tenant. Good man.

[1 1]

NEARLY OUT OF PAPER

Once you had done what you came in to do, then read everything worth reading on the nail and had a bit of a think, there
was no point in hanging around. Besides, some poor soul in desperate need might come dashing down the path at any moment.

We're nearly there, so I will let the last word go now to Beryl
Matthews, whose childhood memories will surely strike a chord
in many hearts.

> The privy was a private place,
> Or so the name would say.
> It stood out in the back yard
> And was used well, every day.
>
> No matter what the weather,
> Be it day or be it night,
> If you found the place was occupied
> You were in an awful plight.
>
> The mainstay was the bucket,
> Galvanised and purpose built;
> You NEVER let it overflow
> Or fill up to the hilt.
>
> 'Twere emptied in the garden
> And made fresh whenever needed;
> And funny thing - our veggies grew
> Though some were never seeded.

I only add one thing to this,
Which now sounds rather sad:
As kids, we had a saying -
Don't go in after Dad!

A Privy By Any Other Name

People have always used the most extraordinary terms to avoid saying precisely where they want to go. There must be hundreds, if not thousands, of euphemisms for the privy. Here are just a few. Is yours included?

Aster room
Backhouse
Biffy
Bogs / Bog house
Bombay
Bush
Chamber of Commerce
Chamberlain's piano (a row of buckets)
Chuggie
Comfort station
Crap-house
Crapper
Crapping castle
Dike
Dinkum-dunny
Dispensary
Doneks
Dubs / Dub house
Duffs
Dunnekin
Dunny
Garderobe

Gong
Grots
Halting station
Heads
Holy of Holies
Honk
House of Commons
House of Office
Houses of Parliament
Hum
Jakes ('Jacques')
Jampot
Japping
Jericho
John
Karzi
Klondike
Larties
Lats
Library
Long drop
Loo
My aunt's / uncle's

Necessary	Tandem (a two-holer)
Netty	The End
Petty	The house where the emperor
Ping-pong house	(or king, etc) goes on foot
Place of ease	The opportunity
Place of repose	The proverbial
Reading room	The usual offices
Round-house	Throne room
Round the back	Thunderbox
Sammy	Watering hole
Shants	Watteries
Shithouse (etc!)	Wee house
Shooting gallery	Widdlehouse
Shot-tower	Windsor Castle
Slash house	Wojamacallit
Smallest room	'Yer tiz'
Sunkie	You know where

A few excuses:

I'm going
- for a Jimmy Riddle
- for a tom tit
- to do something you can't do
  for me
- to pick a daisy
- to powder my nose
- to see a man about a dog
- to shake hands with my
  best friend
- to spend a penny
- to stack the tools
- to telephone Hitler
- to the George
- to the groves
- to turn my bike round
- to wash my hands
- to water my horse
- where the wind is always
  blowing